Prophet's Tale
A Life in the Life of an Orphan

By Prophet Dauda

To my beloved late mother Gladys Kadzuwa (RIP), my sponsors Tom and Kristin Podgorski, my grandmother Ethel Dymon, Kathy Stagg Ward and the entire Passion Center Family

Many thanks to the following people for all the efforts they put forward to make this work what it is today: Pastor Eric Von Barnau Sythoff, Patricia Erdmann, Shannon Criswell and Brad Criswell.

FOREWORD

The story of an orphan, be it their plight or successes, is often told by people or groups that champion the cause of orphans. Little do we hear from the orphan himself.

In "Prophet's Tale," Prophet Dauda shares his own experience from his plight as an orphan and how his life changed for the better – an intriguing example of beauty from ashes.

In his book, Prophet brings together the rare combination of his writing skills, which he obtained from college and had become his passion, and a real personal experience.

Prophet recounts how he grew up without knowing his father's love and provision. Before his father died, he was incarcerated and Prophet did not know him. When he was released he went to live in another town and did not make any effort to come and see his children. Prophet and his family were bound in poverty and pain and life became even harder when his mother died. Prophet and his blood brothers and sister were finally taken in by their grandmother, who herself had no source of income.

Prophet recounts how the trajectory of his life was changed when men and women of faith joined hands to support him and many others in his village and other surrounding villages in the name of Jesus through a ministry called the Passion Center for Children in Zomba, Malawi.

In his book, what he calls "the brighter day" is when he was accepted to go to university. For an orphan, this is not a small thing; it was a bright day indeed.

In school, Prophet loved History and especially English. This is where he got excited about writing and he wanted to tell the world about his story – not to make a name for himself but to be an encouragement to other orphans and play his small part in championing their cause. His story is one of those beautiful stories that encourage every reader that every bit of their support goes a long way. He was one of the few who were given an opportunity and he utilized it.

Prophet concludes his story with a powerful statement, affirming the staggering statistics all around the world regarding the many orphans who need to be given an opportunity similar to what he received, and he urges us to act.

The best way to help an orphan is to teach him how to "fish." For Prophet, the opportunity to receive assistance towards his primary school through to university (besides the spiritual guidance and many other basic needs) was the turning point in his life.

Pilira W. Chibwana
National Director, Passion Center Malawi
Rev.

Part One

Misty Morning

The solution to poverty in our societies lies right inside our very minds and hearts. The outside is just there to set a stepping stone. Today, Africa and many other Third World countries are still yoked in poverty since the attainment of independence because an opportunity that is laid by the First World or any well-wisher is mistaken for a solution.

CHAPTER ONE

The center that does not hold

Neither my father and mother nor my brothers and sisters had a diary recording our family experiences. In fact, my family never valued such things. As long as we ate and moved on to the next sunrise, everything was fine.

My clan-people may be well-known for the art of Orality which passes from this generation to the other. The Orality that sings and tells-*'why the hare has upright ears'*-`*why women carry children on their backs'*-*'why a cat and rat are great enemies'*-and many others. The irony is that most children of our compound grew up without knowing their own family histories. Is it a taboo in our compound to tell a child what his or her family has been through in the past decade? In the city, maybe children are told, or maybe not.

I grew up not seeing a father. On one or more occasions a certain senior man of our compound had talked about my father in a drunken state. Something I noted among the drunkards of my village, even of other villages, was this: they either liked to show off that they knew a word or two in English or had a well-grounded knowledge about certain people or things. The senior man staggered on that clear sky afternoon. He saw me.

'Yes, your mom,' he began out of nowhere, 'was married to a driver in the government. A policeman.' He spoke with an impression that my father was a great man. I am sure he was a blood relative, though a year or so later, I never saw him again. If I say that I know what happened to this man, then honestly it is going to be one-hundred-percent pure guesswork.

Of course the bits and pieces of his story about my father carried a considerable sense that my father was a great man. But with the fact that I never had a chance to meet him, there was no way I was going to appreciate his greatness and even a father-son tie that existed between us. In this life, we forget to pay attention to hypocrisy that lies behind every good thing. In our daily life, for instance, I hear people say, "This land has a good water or oil reserves," but seldom do people look at how many people, in that land, benefit from those water or oil reserves.

The senior man's scraps made a clear sense only when my brothers and sisters told me why I did not see my father. I learnt the story when I got to the university and it took tricky questioning for them to reveal it. I had known that every child must have a biological father, so where was mine?

I wanted to know about the man who gave me a suit which my mother used to hang on the wall. She said that the brown suit was my gift from my father. Most of the time it just stood lifeless as it gathered dust on the wall. In fact it was big, so big that a tailor could make four or five sets of shorts for my small body from a single leg of the trousers. As a child, I just enjoyed the sense of ownership mostly brought by mother every time she saw me looking at the suit from a distance as I hoped that one day my small body would grow into it and put it on.

This sense of ownership was at once taken away for a lifetime when the harvest moon appeared. The third oldest man of our compound borrowed it when he was invited to a traditional feast in a distant compound. My mother, without my consent, gave it to him. Since then he endlessly borrowed it as he attended more traditional feats. My suit began losing thread after thread until to the very last thread.

I clearly recall my brothers' and sisters' explanation: `It was in the 1990s. Our family was transported in a government car from Lilongwe Area 30 to here, our village. Our father's hands and legs were in shackles sitting in the middle of a few policemen armed to the teeth. Us and mother, then expectant, sat on one side of the car with the family belongings. 'For you,' my brother said pointing at me. `You were happily swimming in her amniotic fluid.'

Unofficially, I was born on the 30th of July, 1994 at Zomba Central Hospital. I say unofficially because seldom, as I said before, did my people record historical occasions. Most parents traditionally kept dates of birth for their children, and so did my mother. Two or three times my mother told me about it. If someone asked your age, you had to consult your parents or any other responsible elder of your compound.

I one-hundred-percent remember, she could not read ABC or count 1-2-3 but, she was good at knowing the dates of birth of her children and the months of rainfall and the harvest season of a year.

Added up, I was the seventh child of Gladys Kadzuwa, for that was the name of my mother. She lived in Thom-Allan Village, Traditional Authority Mwambo in Zomba District. She had a sister Catherine and two half-brothers, Austin and Michael. They all lived in Thom-Allan village with their widowed mother Ethel, whom I regard as *anganga*, grandmother.

My father's story can be best put as 'The Jailer who got jailed.' His name, as I was told by his ageing father, was Austin Amman Dauda from Chikwekwe Village, Traditional Authority Mwambo, Zomba District. He had been a police officer until he got arrested and sent to the Zomba Maximum Security Prison and he lost his job.

We were born seven of us: Charles, Jane, Getrude, Mercy, Sunganani, Godfrey, and I, Prophet, (or Proph) the last.

I reached an age when I was able to solve a few puzzling riddles and proverbs of our clan. I may not be sure, but I guess I was between 4 and 6. I had good friends within the compound and it was good. But there was one thing that I could not understand as a child. My friends-Chifuniro (Uncle Austin's last born); Alice (Auntie Catherine's last born); the clever Phuzo and many more-had someone to call a father. I saw my friends were privileged just by having someone to call a 'father.'

Despite the fact that my father died in 1999, as a kid, I was still questioning myself why I had not seen him in our compound, for he got released out of prison. I had been ignorant of his whereabouts until my brothers and sisters told me as I said before. It is also through them that I knew a step my father took after his release from prison. It was a sad story for my poor mother. It was a wave of scratches on her heart. As soon as he got released he left my mother for another woman in the neighboring busy town, Blantyre. It would be empty of me if I say, it was a divorce.

Though I grew up not knowing what having a father was like, I knew fathers had a world of their own which made them champions and gods over the rest of the family members. I observed this from some men who fathered children in our compound. A father had the final say, a father did not make mistakes, no one could question his authority, a wife had to serve him, and he deserved the best portion of food.

So no doubt my father drew his energy from such a masculine world and abandoned my mother. My father's move delivered my mother to the powerful jaws of the harsh matrilineal customary law of the Southerners. In my clan it is widely held that: all children belong to the mother's side. This left the poor woman in a deep state of poverty. The only thing her people trained her for a living was to hold on to a hoe until her death-knell would sound. Sometimes our native customary laws, such as the Southern Matrilineal System, have created a fertile ground on which our societies stand to burden our women. The customary laws blind the societies so that an abnormality becomes a normal thing. When a woman's heart is cracked under the customary law everything turns out normal, so normal that people resume a normal life as if nothing has happened.

Our house was located on one end of the full moon-shaped compound. The house was built with sun-dried bricks and roofed with some rusty and holed iron sheets. These were donated by my uncle, Mr. Mphonda, a famous village trader.

He was also the owner of the lineage of our family line, *Mwinimbumba*. Old mats and sackcloth were used when no glasses were available for windows.

If one entered the house, they would be greeted by a spacious room that served as a living room. In one corner we kept our plates, cups and a few earthen pots. There were some chairs made of dried creepers and a neatly packed bookshelf that was partly eaten by termites.

There were two inner rooms extending from the living space. The one inner room served as a corral for chickens, a storage room for maize flour and drinking water. It was mostly dark and mosquito-filled. The other room, that's where I, mother, Godfrey and Sunganani slept. It was too small to accommodate seven of us. So Getrude, Mercy and Jane had to be accommodated in some houses that were within the compound. By then Charles was at a boarding school, Nankhunda Minor Seminary, so I am sure my mother could a say a little prayer for that. Still, when a school holiday came for him, he had to be accommodated in *gowelo*, a grown up boys hut, within or outside our compound.

A few meters away from the house stood a grass-thatched cooking hut. It was also built with sun-dried bricks.

CHAPTER TWO

You have no fee, walk in for free

Between 50 and 70 percent of children in our village were going to school. Older boys and girls than me, maybe four years older, were going to Mulunguzi Full Primary School. So did Mercy, Sunganani and Godfrey.

Every morning, mother would wake up with the first cock-crow. She would fry fritters, *mandasi*. She sold them on the road a few meters away from the main entrance to our compound. Our house was close to the main entrance of the compound. The entrance was so close to the main dusty road that connected a distant trading town, Zomba, and Jali.

But if I say that selling *mandasi* was a permanent income-generating activity for her, surely I will be telling a lie. She even switched to being a banana seller, to a sugar cane seller, to a crop seed seller, to a groundnuts seller. Anything. Actually, in my village, even in other surrounding villages, trade items were determined by what the soil gave out in that particular season. If the land gave out groundnuts, it was time to trade in groundnuts; so it was when the land gave out bananas and pumpkins and sugarcane and many others. Every villager in my village, and other villages, strongly believed in being creative with any available resource to hop to the next sunrise.

Her morning would continue by boiling some water to get my brothers and sisters ready for school. After making sure that the chickens were let out, the plates from the previous meal were cleaned, she would take her usual medium-handled hoe to hoe part of the garden that enclosed our house. In total my mother owned two good-sized gardens. Yields from the two gardens could feed us until the next harvest season. But I am not sure if we could feed an extra stomach from our yearly yields.

Kids at my age or younger were attending a nursery school, Tiyeseko Nursery School at the Mkalyainga Residence, on the other side of the dusty road.

Seriously I tell you, life on the other side of the road was different. It was as if the dusty road separated people depending on their social status. Maybe it was a yardstick for the social stratification of the people of the land in which I was raised. On that bank of the road, land was privately owned and leased while on our side, it was publicly owned. On the other bank, there was the Kampeni Residence, Mkalyainga Residence, Meyer Residence, Kalizambeta Residence, Chiona Residence and Chimbalawala Residence.

The residencies were spread all along the road and covered a huge length with their lands. It is with no doubt the owners of these residencies were great people. In my land it is not easy to own land privately because it is widely believed that land belongs to ancestral spirits. Either the current or distant heads of these residences had gone through a white man's education. This was an education that gave them the ability to look at things from a Western angle. The possession of the Western education threw them in the same box with the locals serving in the *boma*, government, of our Great Nation. *Boma* was an administrative system brought to our native land by colonialists from Britain. So they were able to talk the same language with the *boma*, in the negotiation to own the land privately. If the *boma* said `A' they were able to carry on to `B' and `C' and `D' on the private land ownership negotiations. But the people on both banks were under the authority of the village headman, Thom-Allan.

Our compound faced the Mkalyainga residence. Every morning I would hear: `Alphabet letters! Twenty six letters!' Those were the kids singing after their faithful teacher. `A B C D!' The singing would continue until they reached Z. `Now I know my alphabet!' How about the weekly days' song?

`How many days make a week?' the teacher would ask them in a singing manner.

'Seven days make a week,' the kids would reply in chorus. 'Sunday! Monday! Tuesday! Wednesday! Thursday! Friday! And Saturday!'

And how about the monthly calendar song? 'Calendar!! Calendar!!' the teacher would continue.

'I know my calendar!' the kids sung again. They would mention all the months of a year in order by heart. 'Round, round like a ball!,' they would finish proudly.

Hearing kids of my age singing, I always told myself, 'This is a great singing.' I wished I could join them, but it was a private school. At the end of every wish I would also tell myself, 'My mother's hoe produces nothing except our yearly yields, not enough to sell and pay for my school so that I can join the great singing.'

On many occasions I had tried to follow my brothers and sister on their way to the public school. But they would either run, or play tricks, or my mother would beat me to stop me from following them.

In fact, my right hand could not reach across my head to my left ear. It was a sign that I was not mature enough to go into primary school.

I remember one morning I had made her look like a careless woman when a certain man nearly hit me with his bike as I was following my brothers to school. 'Is your mother tired of you?'

the angry man shouted. 'Or else she is going to have another baby after you are hit!' His eyes were bloodshot.

'There is a masked dancer or a big animal there', my mother would scare me to turn back while hoeing in the garden. So after turning back, I could sit beside where my mother sold her items. I was on watch for the buyers as she worked in the nearby garden. *'Ama, kwabwera anthu!'* I could shout out when a buyer came. By then I did not know any calculations to do with money. But my recall is as clear as in a picture; an item could go at one kwacha or two kwacha or less, only I had no idea of what the coins looked like.

One kwacha or less, today, sounds like not enough to buy an item and you might laugh. But in our day, it had weight. Those were the old sweet days of my great nation!

What was I saying? Yes…*'Ndikubwera!'* she would reply while leaving her hoe to attend to the buyer. After assisting the buyer, she would keep the money under the sack-cloth on which the items were displayed. She could resume with hoeing and I, too, would resume waiting for more buyers.

Days were passing by. Every morning I admired the singing and loved to, from a distance, watch as the pupils rode on small three-wheeled bikes, playing soccer and sitting on the see-saw, moving up and down.

One morning, as usual, my mother was hoeing. This morning, she did not display items for sale. She did not fry the fritters and the bananas were not ripe in an earthen pot filled with maize bran. So I went to play in the garden she was hoeing. One or two times I chased grasshoppers that had leapt from old stalks she cut and heaped in one place before setting fire to them.

'My grasshopper,' I would say while chasing one that flew towards the banana trees. I had a thin stalk of grass in my hands.

'I told you to stop. You hear well when a hand has been laid on you!' she shouted. 'Can't...'

'How are you? So he is happy hunting grasshoppers instead of being in school?' she was interrupted by a voice from the road. It was Mrs. Kapindura, the owner of Tiyeseko Nursery School. She was also a secondary school teacher in town. I knew her well as the mother to my good friend Emma.

'You! What are you doing?' she asked at the same time pointing at me. I became deathly still embarrassed. I did not know whether she really expected an answer because she had seen me chasing the insects with a stick in my hands. Was it only to show that she was concerned about me? I did not know.

'I am not selling much these days,' my mother replied while still holding the hoe.

'He should join school,' she said at last after they had talked over a few things which I could not really figure out. The only thing I saw was sadness that was written all over my mother's face. Poor woman. I felt sorry for her. Her circumstance left her an unconfident and insecure woman, always bringing sadness on her face. Today that expression of sadness makes me wonder: if she had known how to read and write, would she be that inferior, always expressed through a sad face?

The two women were close friends. Many times, my mother sent me to deliver something to Mrs. Kapindura in an earthen pot sealed with a cloth. Eventually, our family also received gifts from Mrs. Kapindura. In fact, communalism is one of the ingredients of life among the people of the land I was raised in. We all say, 'I exist because we exist.'

In the evening, Mrs. Kapindura called me to her house. It was as if I was in a dream.

'Tomorrow start coming here,' she said while offering me a shirt. I examined it with my eyes, very excited, to see whether or not it would come down just below my buttocks. My one and only shirt was bare-thread in the back. I later learnt that I was the only child to attend the school for free.

'Sweet, escort your friend,' she said to Emma who by then was standing next to me.

Emma carried my shirt in a medium plastic sack. I told her not to cross over to our side due to the gathering dusk. I assured her that I would see her tomorrow. Actually, she could have come with me to our house. It was not about the gathering dusk but to let her go so that I could rush to my mother and brothers and sisters to show off my new shirt. I was excited like a kid who has never tasted sweets, but on the road meets a generous person who gives him sweets but he can only eat it when he gets home. So imagine the excitement that fills such a kid on the way home. Such excitement filled me.

So Emma went back. Honestly, she took after the beauty of her mother. I often thought about that. She was perfectly formed with a medium height and thickness and light skinned. But I was a little taller than her.

I ran towards my mother with happiness. I showed her my new shirt and tried it with different walking styles across the spacious room of our house. My brothers admired me.

'Tomorrow, school,' I spoke within myself. In no time, I moved out and spread the news, as a child, to other kids.

The next dawn, I woke up by the first cock-crow. I did not go back to sleep at all until it got clear. My mother bathed me and I put my new shirt on. I could not take my eyes off my new shirt on my body. Although I had no shoes on my feet, I still felt great in my new state. My mother wrapped a fritter in a small plastic sack to eat during a break. I walked over and got to my first school.

I tell you, to sit among those singing kids and sing with them, was not just a common thing. Even heavens know that I single it out as one of my happiest hours and days in my life ever.

CHAPTER THREE

I sing, read and play with them

Each weekday, I went to the school. Each morning I would wake up. The first thing was to play with antlions that dug round the edge of our house and the cooking hut. At this time my mother would be preparing my brothers and sister for school.

To play with the antlions, I carried a thin stalk of grass and poked in their holes. '*Wooooo!*' That was me as I rotated the stalk into the cone-shaped hole. 'It is out,' said I, as it came out by climbing over the fine sand wearing off the edges of the hole. When I had it, I moved on to the next hole.

After preparing my brothers, my mother washed my body while seated on my buttocks on a flat and medium height rock. It was behind our house.

Half of the kids at the school were from middle class families. And almost eighty percent of the parents of the kids managed shoes, a small backpack, a food container and a drinking bottle. It is in the record of the school history, that I was one of the very few kids who carried their food in plastic sacks and bare feet.

At school, I loved to ride the three-wheeled bike. It would not move by peddling; instead others had to push you. Two of my friends, the same height as me, pushed me and it was really nice.

Of course I took turns with my two male friends in pushing each other. I can wholeheartedly admit that most of my turns to push were aside from the two friends. I liked to push Emma. I could tirelessly push and push and push. I loved the fact that the pushing placed a nice smile on her face, topping up the already existing beauty on her face. God, Emma was perfectly formed. She was a replica of her beautiful mother.

No wonder it drove me into jealousy when Rumbani, another kid, claimed that he was in an affair with her. Up to date I do not know whether he was telling the truth. But his claim sparked a fight and the teacher had to separate us.

Despite his claim, there was something to pull me up. It was something to create confidence in me. Each day after school, my mother told me, 'Go and help that girl cross the road.' By then Emma was said to stand, like an angel, on the edge of the other side. I would stop whatever I was doing and ran towards her and helped her cross to our side.

With other kids, from other compounds and ours, we could play and play and play until the sun went down on the horizon. Our playing ranged from games such as hide-and-seek, football and even tagging games. At times we made play houses in the bush. In these, some male kids pretended to be husbands while female kids acted as wives. At times, male kids outnumbered female kids so those who weren't husbands acted as hyenas or roosters or watchmen or thieves. These were the lowest roles one could play during play houses. They were mostly associated with kids who did not have much influence to the group.

The hyenas went about on four legs barking, scaring our childish world. The watchmen carried sticks and wrestled against the thieves who tried to break into the huts of grass stalks and dried banana leaves. The roosters too, played their role. They were kept in one corner where they crowed, marking the break of the dawn. When they crowed, the husbands and the wives in the huts were supposed to come out and do their chores as people do in day time. There was a funny story about a certain boy who grumbled on being chosen as a rooster. In fact, a girl that this boy liked so much was taken by another boy. So a wonderful plan struck him. He crowed minute after minute.

In our play houses, a husband and wife lived like a real family. I recall we would bring some old mats and share a bed on them. I remember as a family we would move beyond our childish world and do what married people do. I remember my mother once caught us doing the 'things that a wife and a husband do.' She warned us never to do the 'foolish thing' again or else she was going to burn our mouths.

Days hatched into weeks, and weeks into months. I had mastered the Week Days song, the Alphabet song and the Calendar song. I also loved this song:

> *Anthu osaphunzira!*
> *Kwawo m'kunyada!*
> *Atenga Pensulo!*
> *Ayika Pamutu*
> *Kulemba Sadziwa*
> *Oh! Zachisoni!*
> *Eh Taona. Eh anzako!*
> *Kunyadira Sukulu Yapamwamba!!!!*

Every time I got home, I practiced the songs before my mother. She liked to hear me singing songs in English though she, herself, did not know what the songs meant. Honestly, no matter how uneducated a parent may be, he or she is always happy seeing his or her children picking up a good pace in learning English.

Not surprisingly a few days later, she found a food container for me. I clearly remember it was red in colour with a white, round lid. It was bought from some barter-traders who used to move out in villages. Actually these traders brought many items that people in the villages lacked. They would either bring salt, sugar or containers and exchanged them for old cooking pots, old umbrellas, old shoes, old bottles and many things.

So my mother did a barter-trade and got the container. The day it was found was a great day. I looked at it. I touched it while seated, standing and seated again. I wished it was morning and I could carry it, with a fritter in it, to school.

At night, after supper, we hung around a family fire. As a compound we came together and ate from a communal dish. My people believed that a man must gather together with his neighbors and eat from the same dish. As children we ate from one plate. So did our mothers.

There was one funny thing that I noted about eating from one plate as children. Those plates with foolish flower decorations on them could betray you. With the darkness you could think you still had relish in the plate without knowing it was those flower decorations. So you would have false hopes from the flowers. At last, you could move your hand with energy to grab the relish only to realize it was those flower decorations. You could feel greatly betrayed.

After eating, still at the fireside, my grandmother would start, `shall I tell you a story?'

`Tell us,' we would reply.

`A long long time ago,' she would begin her narration.

I called such times `tale times'. I loved tales about animals, especially the clever Hare. There was one tale about how the clever Hare fooled a hyena when they went out to propose to some beautiful girls in one of the surrounding villages. This tale made me laugh and laugh and laugh until my stomach ached. In fact, time and again I asked my mother to re-narrate it to me. Actually, from the animal tales which my grandmother, mother, brothers and sisters told me, I had the impression that the hare was the cleverest animal in the bush. What about those tales about how the same Hare fooled the king Lion and an elephant?

On a night like this, when the moon was full, the youth from our compound went out to the playground. The playground was outside of the compound. They sang, danced and played games with other youth from neighboring compounds.

`*Goo! Go di di...! Kapamba yako sikadyakena...!*' Either the drum beat echo or their singing echo could penetrate the calm air in the full moon. Every time a car drove through the dusty road, they ran towards it singing. They were excited to see their shadows reflected on the mud walls of nearby houses. Lights from the cars reflected their shadows on the mud walls. And they sang:

Iwe falodi!!!
Makutu akowo!!!
Kuwomba bobo!!
Bobobo!!!!!!!!

CHAPTER FOUR

I must have a biological father. Yes.

Years passed. My father had not appeared in our compound. By then, though I knew it when I got to university, he was released from prison. After his release he left our family for good and went to Blantyre where he had found a new job, in the Ministry of Education. And he never found a single minute to pay us a visit in our `prison.'

Yes, our `prison.' I do get it when an Ethiopian writer, Harma Tuma, writes `your house can be your prison.' Out there in our societies poverty has created a prison. The law sentenced my father to imprisonment by throwing him into a thick and barbed-wire fenced building. At the same time his imprisonment sentenced us to a prison of poverty. A prison whose walls are invisible but all its prisoners have a special chain or shackle, making the prisoners visible to onlookers as some struggle to free themselves from the chains. But some have been silenced by the power of the chains and hopeless they have grown. They just await the sound of their death-knell as their `world' gets dark, darker and darkest.

My father grew stronger economically in the new city. Still, he never spared even a single second to peep his eyes through to see how we were struggling against the yoke of poverty.

One day, something unusual happened in our home. It was morning. The sun was rising over the horizon in the east. The sky was perfectly clear. My mother bathed me. And she made sure Godfrey and Mercy and Sunganani were prepared, too. I was told I was going to see my father at Chancellor College, an arm of the University of Malawi. It stood maybe ten minutes walking-distance from my home. There was a graduation ceremony, so some people from the Ministry of Education were going to attend. My father was attending too.

It seemed a great day for me. I was, just like any child, very excited. I developed confidence in him right away. As a child I observed that a father was a knot to which all the family members were tied to. He was a center-pole of the family. If a child misbehaved a mother would report to the father. And if a child felt intimidated, it would run to the father for protection. At my age, I was able to know that I was supposed to have a biological father to be our center-pole and my protection. So the story about meeting my father sent me into a confident kid.

Another thing that stirred my excitement on that morning was that the popular Dr. Bakili Muluzi was also going to be there. By then, just like every child in our village, I knew him as the leader of our Great Nation. Faithful followers of his party fondly called him `Atcheya.' A million times I heard the radio, the National Crier, announce `*Atcheya Woyeeee!*' and others replied `*Woyeeeee!*'

I clearly recall, previously, two or three times he had landed his planes on Chirunga ground. As children we always got excited with the planes. We would run into nearby bushes as the planes landed with great noise. After the landing, I and other dirty children I didn't know would sneak out of the bushes and wave at him. In turn he smiled at us and waved back. Maybe a wave and a smile were enough for these ragged kids and a million others in other villages.

I have not forgotten that at one point he looked straight at me and gave me a wave. I felt so great and innocently wore a smiling face all day, even after he left.

`Maybe he is going to wave at me again,' I kept telling myself as my mother helped put on my shirt from Mrs. Kapindura. By then it had lost some threads and it had begun exposing my body. In fact since it was given to me, it rarely left my body. Any new cloth becomes far better than the old one. So as a kid I strongly insisted on putting it on all the time.

We were set to go. Mercy carried an old wrapper, partly worn out. This was to carry me with on her back in case I got tired of walking.

'Tell your father we have nothing to lean on,' my mother strongly repeated into Mercy's ears. She emphasized not forgetting to relay the message. 'The rains will start failing soon,' she continued. We stood still looking at her. 'The two gardens are tilled. Tell him. But fertilizer is needed. So tell him.'

In no time we were on the dusty road heading up. About fifteen minutes later, we came to the huge buildings. I had never seen such buildings before. The buildings were carefully roofed and very tall. So much taller than that of Kampeni Residence and the Mkalyainga Residence and the Meyer Residence and the Kalizambeta Residence and the Chiona Residence and the Chimbalawala Residence.

The huge buildings had electricity. The small roads that branched from the buildings were tarred and clean.

Our feet had been covered with dust for we had used the dusty road. We had to wipe off the dust from our legs. Mercy wiped mine with the wrapper as she shouted at me. She shouted at me because a million times I had turned down her offer to carry me on her back as we were coming.

'I am walking on my own. And I am not tired yet.' I had replied that way when she offered to carry me.

There were many cars enclosing one huge building. This one might have been described as the mother building at Chancellor College. This was the Great Hall where the graduation ceremony was taking place.

My sister recognized my father's car. To date, I cannot tell for sure whether it belonged to him. We went straight to it. We spread out the wrapper and sat on it. Hopefully, my father was going to come out, greet us and maybe carry me in his hands too. And maybe buy us food, for we did not bring any. We just ate some boiled cassava before we started off.

As we were seated, I saw clean and well-dressed children at a distance. They were talking to either their mothers or fathers in English. I admired them and thought of Tiyeseko Nursery in our village.

'They must be kids of great schools in town,' I thought. It created inquisitiveness in me. I also thought of a future day when I would be able to speak English like these town kids.

The sun had now risen in the sky. Soon it was going to hang overhead. My father was still nowhere to be seen. My inward center of hope began to grow weak and weaker and weakest. My brothers had twice or so tried to search for him around the corridors branching to and from the Great Hall. My sister had strongly cautioned them to be more careful or else they might get lost because the people were many, so many so that even an ant could not see where to crawl.

All over people were sitting in pairs or small groups eating their lunch. These were westernized families. It was not the way we used to eat in our compound. Here there was no such thing as 'a man must call around his neighbors to eat from the same round-flat basket.' The people were opening their lunch boxes. As they did, a good smell escaped from the lunch boxes.

It was a strange, delicious smell to me and I had never eaten food with such a smell since I was born. And two or three times, my sister had rebuked me, to my face, for looking at their mouths as they ate. But I know you might understand the reaction of a kid in my situation when such delicious smell gets mixed with the oxygen he is inhaling. Moreover, I had gone without food since we got to the place.

'You don't hear at once,' said she while punching my mouth, my lips having developed stiff cracks due to thirst and hunger. 'Looking people in the mouth as they eat as if you don't eat at home. You are embarrassing us,' she continued.

I honestly hated her for what she was saying. Was she hypocritical? I wanted to cry out loud but I quickly went against it. But my eyes were filled with tiny streams of tears.

Instead, out of nowhere, I began developing hatred toward my father. Within seconds, hate was filling up my heart at the rate a water pipe, at full pressure, fills a small container. As I am writing these lines, I do not know how to put it. Since I was born, it was my first time to develop strong hatred towards someone, and for that matter, my own father. My mind's eye saw the knot which was supposed to tie my family together held loose. I saw a man in the name of my father grow into a stranger in my life. And with passage of time, he completely grew faint in my young life.

The third attempt by my brothers to search for him was successful. Not because they found the stranger, but a certain unknown woman offered them three samosas. She was about to throw them to a trash can because she thought they would go bad if not eaten soon. So she beckoned at my brothers from her car window and handed them the samosas. They brought them and we ate them. The way I was hungry, my stomach would not really understand the woman saying they were going bad. I licked my hands clean and accompanied my last chew with cold water from a nearby pipe. This woman was worth calling `my father.'

Yes, 'my father.' Was my biological father not going to feed me? Here, out of kindness, she fed my hungry stomach. Honestly, this woman's kindness, young as I was, made my life came across an expensive discovery about women. Kindness is the most womanish of a woman. The story of my life unfolds from a strong foundation laid by women I met at a tender age. Was my first shirt for school not from a woman? Was I not offered free education by a woman in her school? Even in later stages of my life, women were a common sight where my life grew hopeless. I will tell you as I go ahead.

In fact the kindness of a woman makes my life understand why the Creator gave her a womb, the place where human life begins. Today in my silent moments, I understand why the world should abandon a backward mindset that a woman cannot play an important role in a society. No, a woman has all the potential just as a man. I can testify to that with energy. Women took courage and laid a very strong foundation for my young life. My father, overpowered by cowardice, shunned this responsibility and flushed himself out of my life.

After gaining strength, we started back home. I did not meet my father. Today, when I look back to this hard day, a day my eyes got soaked when I saw my brothers helplessly searching for my father, my mind has discovered one secret about this life. Sometimes it is good to move on as if nothing has happened. Life is about moving forward. A man who spends all his energy thinking about yesterday is foolish and cowardly. Our yesterday is full of misery and mistakes that can only be corrected with our focus on what comes next.

Later, on the 12th of May, 1999, I heard that my father had passed on after a short illness. My mother, just like any other southern woman, in the manner of a widow, mourned. She tied her head in a cloth and mourned. The same youthful innocence I had before he died blinded me to the mourning shadow that fell across our family. Honestly, I did not cry for him. If I shed tears, it was because my mother shed tears, too. I will never call my mother empty for crying for my father. I respect the fact that this was a woman who made a sacred vow to live with her husband as one body until death separated them. And this vow was powerful, but not powerful enough to not be broken by the man who left unexpectedly before neither of them breathed their last.

And the mourning atmosphere was exactly, in my senses, the same which the land wore when a stranger in another corner of the land had died.

CHAPTER FIVE

A newcomer at public school

The later months of 1999 marked nine months I had spent at Tiyeseko Nursery School. This was according to the academic calendar in those days.

It was now the closing day of the 1999 academic year. Unfortunately I was feeling a bit under the weather. It was malaria in its early stage. So my mother suggested I lay on an old mat in our house. Every child's parent went to the closing ceremony, and so did my mother.

'*Lulululu!!!,*' I could hear women ululating. '*Phwa! Phwa!*' the cries of joy could be followed by hands being put together. I was debating within myself whether to wake up. But I went against it.

Before the sun reached its zenith in the sky, the ceremony was over. My mother came back carrying a pencil, notebook and some biscuits. These were my congratulatory gifts. Out of all children, I came in position one. Like a sleeping hare awakened by hunting dogs, I sprang from the old mat and took my gifts from her hands.

'Mine?' I asked, already knowing the answer.

'Yes. Yours,' she replied with a smile.

'Why did they give it to me?' I pompously asked as a child.

'You were in position one,' she endured my rhetoric.

I touched them and wished the next academic year could start right there. Again and again I touched and looked at my gifts while standing, sitting and lying on my back on the mat. *I will have a great day at Mulunguzi Full Primary School!* was the only thought my mind had.

'Are you going to use them today?' my mother came out strongly. She looked at how long I had kept the gifts in my hands. 'They are either going to get damaged or lost before your school starts.' She moved on. I remained silent.

The rainy season came. It started with early rains, and the main rains. People planted. Now the green maize stalks were about knee-high in the gardens. It was green throughout. This was the New Year of 2000. Within the same month of January, schools were going to open. Do not forget, this was the year I was going to attend my first public school, Mulunguzi Full Primary School.

My mother worked hard to buy some resources for me, for my school. She secured part-time work doing weeding in a few surrounding gardens. This is what was happening. In the morning as a family we hoed in our family garden.

One thing she made sure of was that all her children knew how to hold a hoe. In fact, in the whole land that was the duty of every parent. My mother bought me a small-handled hoe. I could not make a good ridge so my brothers and sisters had to give me an example until I mastered making a ridge or weeding or banding on my own.

In the evenings, my mother worked in the other gardens. She sourced enough money to buy shoes for me. I should say my first shoes.

So one day, my mother sent me to the trading town. I went with my sister, Jane. In those days, a good shoe could go at one-hundred kwacha. We carried that same amount of money. Had it been that I had shoes before, my sister would have just gone on her own and selected a pair in my size. But these were going to be my first shoes since I was born. So I had to go, too, and try different sizes and buy the ones that fit me. And of course get to know my shoe size from the one that fit me.

In those days, the shoes that were in fashion were some plastic shoes fondly called 'Tobi.' Honestly, I do not know why they had that name. If you ask someone like me, who witnessed this fashion, there were one or two things to say about these shoes. They stood a taste of time. A single pair could be passed down to other family members. My brother once had a pair that he passed down to Jane, who passed it down to Getrude, who passed it down to Mercy, who passed it down to Sunganani. By the time it got to Sunganani, the shoelaces had worn out and were replaced with wild strings. But the shoes still looked strong as if they were bought yesterday. Actually, I observed that those Tobi shoes had an unclear ending. They were either abandoned to an ash-heap or under a tree before children used them as car toys. The children drove them on the ground by hand or a stick.

Secondly, they had sharp edges that would dig deep into your ankle every time you had them on. I remember that when someone wore them on a journey, they would reach their destination hanging them around their shoulders. This was so because you took them off due to too much pain in the ankles. If you were to wear them for the whole day, you were surely going to cut through your ankle.

Still, no matter how much your ankle bled, the good thing was that you were in shoes, a thing not common to the children of our time.

At the town, all the shoes seemed a little smaller or larger than my feet. So we had no choice. My sister suggested taking a pair into which I was going to be fitting some rags in front before fitting my feet. This was to give a tight fit when I got them on my feet.

Day came and it was morning. My mother woke up, as usual, at the crow of the cock and high tone of prayer from the town mosque. She filled up a hip-high drum with water from a public pipe. The pipe was located outside our compound, but at a distance. She also filled the earthen pot kept in the cooking hut.

Soon the birds sang merrily, marking the day break. The birds whistled from tall trees that stood in a semi-circle near our house.

My brothers and sister took their baths. My mother sliced my notebook into two equal halves. This was the notebook I received on the closing day at Tiyeseko Nursery School. The pencil, too, was sliced into several pieces. If I were to lose a pencil or a notebook on my first day I would still have some left. She was a Prophetess in that regard. I will tell you as we go ahead.

This morning I did not play with the antlions. Instead I stood next to my mother with my uncovered stomach. I was caught with a strange nervousness to go to a new school and to get to meet new learners and teachers. It was the kind of nervousness that catches you when you are travelling alone to a distant place you have never been before.

After eating some boiled bananas with salt, we headed east along the dusty road. From the east the red sun was rising. Children walked in small groups as they walked to school. Actually, the dusty road was always busy during mornings. It was full of children in their bands on their way to school, workers on their way to town, and other villagers branching out in all directions to their gardens.

The majority of continuing students were dressed in their school uniforms. Boys put on black shorts and a blue shirt. And girls put on a long, blue dress with a pink collar. My sister and brothers were in their uniforms, too. My sister was by then in Standard Five while my brothers were in Standard Three.

But if one extended eyes down the feet of these students, their feet were bare. No shoes on them. They had no shoes, not because they did not want to put them on but their parents were peasants and a shoe was a luxury. Not wearing a shoe was an abnormal thing that turned out to be normal to them. Actually I observed that a shoe did not bring a new day in the kids' lives. Be it in shoes or not, all the days were the same. A face that a kid wore when in shoes was all the same he wore when not in shoes. Was it because of the pain from the sharp edges of the shoes? Was it because the majority of the students were bare feet? Sometimes when a wrong habit is practiced by the majority, it may seem as a right habit.

As we walked, my sister's hand held mine and she also carried my writing materials for me. The way I walked, it was as if she dragged me to hurry up. In fact I was being careful with my steps because my new shoes, as I have already pointed out, were cutting into the lower part of my ankle. I felt a sharp pain every time I moved my feet.

We arrived at my new school after a long walk. I might say so because it was my first time to go that distance. You might understand how much travelling a road for the first time might seem longer, but as days and years went by, the same distance grew shorter because I got used to it.

True, it was a new school, different from Tiyeseko. There were big boys and big girls dressed in their uniforms. I did not expect a school to have such big students.

Mulunguzi Full Primary School had, in total, four classrooms. Only three were complete and the fourth one was at window level. There were a few sheds built with poles and old maize stalks, dried banana leaves or grass stalks. These sheds supplemented the inadequate classrooms. There were also two other buildings, the Headteacher's office and a church, under the Church of Central Africa Presbyterian (CCAP). The church was on one end of the schoolyard. The church was also used as a classroom at times. The Headmaster's office had one shelf that shelved the very few textbooks that the school had. The school had two boreholes, underground water pumps, *mjigo*, for water. This was not a common thing to other schools. To have even one *mjigo* was a far-fetched dream for other nearby schools. So it was something we were to be proud of.

Outside, it was green throughout, being the rainy season. There were also trees that topped up the green scenery. On one tree an old piece of timber had been nailed. The wood had the school's mission statement "WE SHALL ALWAYS CREATE A CONDUCIVE LEARNING ENVIRONMENT FOR A TEACHER AND A LEARNER SO AS TO ACHIEVE QUALITY EDUCATION."

On a distant tree, below one of its branches, a sonorous gong dangled. It was a school bell and on Sundays it served as the church bell too.

A few minutes later, one grown up boy hit the gong with another metal.

'Ngo! Ngo! Ngo!' The echo pierced the cold, calm air which enveloped the school on that morning. The echo sent the students running. And they criss-crossed each other as they ran to the open ground in the middle of the school. The buildings stood in a rectangle, giving space in the middle.

In the open space morning assemblies were conducted. The Headmaster, Mr. Kanyundo, and other teachers addressed the students after singing the National Anthem and reciting a few prayers. The Anthem and the prayers did not make sense, as it was my first time hearing them. At times, in the course of singing, I just moved my lips as if I was singing with them.

At the end of the assembly, grown-up students, from Standard Five to Eight, were told to bring hoes and machetes. Students from Standard One to Standard Four were told to bring brooms.

CHAPTER SIX

The adjusting

The first week of the term was wholly dedicated to general cleaning. Older students cut and slashed down the green plants that had sprouted with the rains.

One group of big boys erected new learning sheds. They also maintained the old sheds that stood in bent positions, nearly brought down by the rains and termites.

Another group maintained an old bridge of poles. Our school stood along the famous Mulunguzi River which ran down from the Zomba plateau. Some students and teachers were either from Matawale homes or villages next to Matawale, and they had to cross to a bank where the school stood. The boys tied the poles tightly with strong creepers. They also used nails on big poles.

Tall grass and other plants that bordered main paths to the school were brought down. It was clear throughout.

Much learning began in the second week. Each morning, when the sun had risen a little, the bell man rang the sonorous gong. The bell man later I learnt was a Head Boy. Always the gong's echo sent us running towards the assembly space.

I clearly remember, as we ran we could scurry in the same way the ants that had been pulling a bit of food collectively ran for safety after sensing danger. Some kids, the same height as me, would fall down as they ran and they cried.

'Up! Down!' A teacher would stand in front and direct us to move our hands in the direction he or she ordered. Some teachers would either stand somewhere among us or move around the lines with a heavy stick. They landed the stick on anyone who did not do what the teacher in front demanded.

In the first days, I was having problems following what the front teacher ordered. I remember on one morning one teacher nearly landed the stick on my head.

'You!' he shouted. It caught the attention of everyone. I was nervous. 'You think you are here to play? If you feel that you are not mature enough for this school go back home. Continue sucking from your mother's breast!' he said fiercely. His voice set fear in me. 'Do as everyone is doing!' he added while walking away.

'Sideways! Forward!' the teacher in front continued, and the students did what he commanded. On a cold day, like this one, the teacher also continued, 'Breathe in! Breathe out!'

Then a senior student was invited to the front to lead a prayer and the National Anthem.

'Unless the Lord builds the house,' he began

'The builders labour in vain,' answered us.

'Our father which art in heaven,' he led the Lord's prayer. 'Hallowed be thy name. Thy kingdom come. Thy will be done, as in heaven, so in earth. Give us day by day our daily bread. And forgive us our sins; for we also forgive everyone that is indebted to us. And lead us not into temptation; but deliver us from evil. Amen.' We prayed collectively.

Then we stood still and sang the National Anthem:

> O God bless our land of Malawi,
> Keep it a land of peace,
> Put down each and every enemy,
> Hunger disease, envy.
> Join together all our hearts as one,
> That we may be free from fear.
> Bless our leader, each and everyone,
> And Mother Malawi.

After the anthem, the Headteacher made announcements. The common one was regarding school uniforms. This, he emphasized.

'As Mulunguzi School we have a uniform, so no need for many colours as if you are chameleons. We will soon start chasing you out of classrooms when you are not putting your uniforms on. For you, new students, Standard One, tell your parents to get you one. If they can't, tell them to keep you in your homes. Those who have just joined us from other schools, make sure you put on uniforms of your previous schools while you are purchasing one for your new school.'

He was a man who knew his job. However, as a student, I took him as a tough man. Maybe it was because I had not put on a school uniform.

Later, as we broke into our classrooms we sang and paraded:

We are walking
In the light of God
Hallelujah!
We are walking
In the light of God.
We are walking!
We are walking!

One of the teachers walked in the lines while commanding 'March!! March!!' At the sight of the heavy stick in his hands, we did a great job with our feet until a huge ball of dust was formed on the ground.

This memory is as fresh as of yesterday: Standard One and Two used to learn under huge trees. The two huge mango trees were within the school yard. On sunny days, their leaves cast a dense shadow. In fact, those leaves were a roof for the under-tree classes.

After each assembly, we would rush and scramble for the stones that we sat on. At times, pupils had to fight as they scrambled for the stones. The oldest boys, class leaders, had to carry a two-legged blackboard. The board was leaned against the huge tree we were sitting under.

I never liked the big boys at all. Apart from carrying the board, they also whipped noise-makers in class. In the course of learning, they could move around the class and even whipped you for moving your lips. They lost their heads with power entrusted to them. It was through the big boys that my young mind learnt that power corrupts men. Students who gave them gifts or knew them were favoured. They were not beaten though they disturbed the class. Ironically, the tough boys endeavored to bring peace in the classroom, though they were the very source of chaos through their power-corrupted minds.

Where there is power violation there is no progress. Our societies cannot move forward if people in authority have lost their heads with power entrusted to them. Minds that are corrupted with power create a fertile ground on which societal chaos breeds.

Sometimes the teacher sent the big boys to nearby potato gardens to pluck the fresh leaves. The leaves were used to clean the board so that the white chalk could be shiny on the board. Weeks later, I learnt that it was a special privilege to do work like fetching the potato leaves. It meant the teacher trusted you. Who does not want to be trusted by his or her teacher?

In our class and in the whole school at large, few students put on school uniforms. It took a month or even a full term for the students' parents to manage a school uniform. People in the surrounding villages were peasants and much of their wealth lay in the soil. If your ancestors chose a fertile land, you were rich. And if your ancestors chose a poor land, you were poor, too.

Some students, especially the grown-ups, would go to a teacher and ask for a job. In return the teacher bought them a school uniform. This included working in the teacher's garden, erecting a grass fence and even cracking firewood.

CHAPTER SEVEN

A tough public school with tough boys

Weeks hatched into months in my new school. I was no longer a stranger but still I had not yet bought my uniform.

I was used to my schedule now. Each morning I would wake up, and as usual my mother rebuked me for wetting my bed.

'Look at you,' she said angrily. 'Don't you realize you are in bed as you urinate?' As she scolded, I mostly behaved as if I was not hearing her.

Instead it sent me into remorse. I thought on how I failed to keep myself from urinating in bed. In the night, I dreamt about chatting with friends. In the course of chatting I often told them I wanted to urinate, and in the process I found myself messing my own beddings. Honestly, I regretted every time I woke up. It pained me.

'You are just clever during the daylight but a fool at night. I will tell your friends that you pee on your own beddings,' she would continue. Revealing it to my friends was seriously going to carry weight.

'*Chikozera Piyo! Piyo!*' my sister and brothers mocked me in a singing manner. In the midst of this humiliation, I resorted to stoning a flock of birds that pecked at some food scraps thrown to the ash-heap behind our cooking hut.

When going to school, I carried my notebook and a pencil in a small plastic sack. My mother had tied a string around the edge of the plastic sack. And every time I walked I just wore it around my neck.

Sometimes, you could see two strings around my neck. The other string held a bottle in which some roasted maize had been soaked. My mother would roast me some maize and soak it all night long. By morning it was softened and easy for me, as a child, to chew. During a short break at school I chewed it.

At times I refused the maize my mother roasted. The big and tough boys snatched it from me mostly. It pained and still pains me because sometimes our yearly maize could not take us to the next harvesting season. I felt it a loss, to take each day, the quantity of the bottle from the little maize and donate it unwillingly to these unkempt boys.

Every time we sang:

Go for break!
Break! Break!
Go for break!

Break! Break!

They stood on their huge stones that they had arranged to act as the door for the un-walled classroom. Peacefully they took my bottle as if we had signed a memorandum of understanding, that every time we sang the break song, they could take my bottle. What flared my anger also was their act after eating. They returned the empty bottle with their faces shining.

'Tomorrow, bring again,' their ring leader would speak. At times I brought my mouth to the edge of the bottle to sip the water in which the maize had been soaked.

It was also no wonder that my pieces of pencil ran out quickly. Each day they stole or forcefully collected pencils from weak students in the class.

I had thought of telling my brothers about it, but every time I was about to, I immediately went against it. I could not even tell our teacher. In fact these tough boys were prepared to drop out of school at any time. When school time came, it was a relief for their parents. Their parents had peace when they were in school.

At school, they were always given corporal punishment. It was part of their routine. It was as if their bodies itched if they were not on corporal punishment. In our day, corporal punishment was allowed in schools. Today, the Human Rights Age has dawned on our Great Nation; corporal punishment in schools is a story of the past. I do not know whether the complete absence of corporal punishment fuels obedient or disobedient behaviours in schools. I say disobedient because I know how sometimes too much of something can spoil a good thing. In our societies we have seen how some people can get spoiled when they have more than what they actually need.

In the midst of humiliation by the big boys, a wonderful plan struck me one day: I must hide my bottle in a nearby bush. That was the plan. I do not know whether I should still call it a wonderful plan because on two or three occasions I found my bottle stolen from the bush in which I had hidden it. It must be the same boys. I was sure about that. In my day, Mulunguzi was a tough public school.

Later, I loved it when my mother began giving me coins. I could easily hide a coin in my shoe. I placed it in front before inserting my feet. At break, I went to a secret bush, untied the shoelace, and took out either my twenty-Tambala or one Kwacha. In my day, when I say money had power, do not think I am cracking a joke. With these coins, we could buy a solid bunch of fruits, even slices of boiled cassava, even boiled bananas, even boiled sweet potatoes, even a considerable piece of an African cake, *chigumu*.

Today our domestic currency has lost power. The fruits, slices of boiled cassava, boiled bananas, boiled sweet potatoes and an African cake are things of a higher price. The future of our domestic currency is determined by the foreign major trading currencies, the US dollar, the British Pound and the Euro. A million times we have seen Kwacha weighed against the US dollar, the Euro and the British Pound. The dilemma is, can Kwacha develop enough weight to stand against the heavy US dollar, British pound and Euro on the balance? Or maybe the owners of Kwacha are not patriotic enough when their currency faces the other currencies? Every time the Kwacha faces a dollar, the Kwacha's power gets lower and lower while the US dollar's power gets higher and higher. And so it is when the Kwacha faces the Euro and the British pound.

On a rainy morning, my mother plucked a fresh banana leaf to act as an umbrella for me. On rainy days, very few students had umbrellas. Where you see one, there were more students than the umbrella could accommodate. Some only sheltered their heads or arms, but the rest of their bodies were soaked. At school, students under the trees learnt in the church due to the rains. So Standard One and Two would become one class on a rainy day.

In school I made friends. Some friends were from our class and others from upper classes.

Some students I knew because we came from the same village. In my class, my friend was Poor Stafford. I call him poor because my shirt had fewer holes than his. Poor Stafford used to live in an old dirty bar with his family. This dirty bar was once owned by my uncle, the trader. It had been subjected to several rainy seasons. It was now a ruin. There were many children in his family.

Another thing I recall about this family is that they went three or four nights without food constantly. But there is this small detail worth sharing about Poor Stafford. He was not stripped. Yes, Poor Stafford was not stripped of his classroom intelligence. He was a solid testimony that sleeping on an empty stomach does not kill your intelligence. He always came in Position One. I could not match my intelligence to his. He was many miles ahead of me and everyone in class. It was sad to see him on other days, missing classes because he was a victim of his circumstance. In our daily lives, people have died with a rich brain because they are either victims of circumstance or they do not have the opportunity to get ahead. Rich and gifted a mind can be, but poverty tries over and over to dilute it and strip it of its gift.

At school, Poor Stafford used to put on his usual white t-shirt. It was very long and stained. This long t-shirt covered his buttocks because the backside of his shorts was threadbare.

I remember other students used to make fun of him for one thing. His mother shaved his head using a razor blade. The razor left him literally with nothing in his head. Because of this, they called him `shiny rock.' This was so because the sun made his head shiny. The tough boys often knocked his head with folded fingers.

Lucky were I and the other students. Our mothers shaved us with scissors. One might laugh on hearing about being shaved with a scissor. Technology has brought innovations in this age and old styles look primitive now. But in our day, it was hard to get a shave with an electric appliance, and there were few barbers in town. It could cost an arm and leg for our parents to send us to a barber in the nearby trading town. So the tough boys did not knock our heads; instead they just mocked us, saying that we had slept on holes of ants that chewed our hair. I did not worry about it as long as they did not beat me.

In school we learnt and learnt and learnt. `My name is,' the teacher made us sing. `I come from…village.' It was all the same, just as at Tiyeseko, so I did not have problems like the other kids who were not privileged enough to attend a nursery school. Where I grew up, it was a privilege to attend a nursery school.

We also learnt Mathematics, how to add and subtract numbers. Before we were done for the day, we would sing songs, tell riddles and tales. Those were old sweet days. I loved the 'London Bridge Song.'

I loved the way we danced it.

> *London Bridge is falling down,*
> *Falling down. Falling down!!*
> *My fair Lady*
> *Lady!!! Lady!!!*

The teacher and one big boy held hands and left space in between them. So we passed under their raised arms while singing the song. Then they trapped some of us with their hands. Then the questioning could begin:

'Where did you go?' the teacher asked.

'Heaven,' replied the trapped students.

'How did you travel?

'By plane.'

'Made by man?'

'No'

'Was it a witch's plane?'

'No.'

'Was it God's plane?'

'*Yessss!!!!!!*"

What did you eat in heaven?'

'*Nsima* with meat'

'Where did you throw the bones?'

'Into a pit'

It went on like that, and we loved to sing it. We did not even know that London was a place. We did not even understand what the song meant. I may also be speaking for the teacher who was leading the song. Later history taught me that London is a place in Britain. And the Britons were once our colonial masters. As kids we innocently sang the song with energy and excitement.

It was the excitement similar to that of the 6th of July, the day which the independence light shone on our Great Nation. On that day, posters about a proud independent Malawi are everywhere in streets. Drums beat and people sing as they dance away into the day. At some point everything comes to a stand-still as we observe a moment of silence in remembrance of the sons and daughters of Malawi whose blood formed a slab on which an independent Malawi stands. Then our right hands rest on the left side of our chests. An expert singer sings the first line of the national anthem and the rest of Malawians follow until the whole anthem is sung.

Today when I equate the excitement from school singing and that of independence, it sparks inquisitiveness in my mind. Have we only pushed out the British rule physically but the colonial authority still exists in our minds? Life has taught me one thing about captivity: if you are chained in captivity, do not think you can liberate yourself physically before you liberate your mind. You can physically break the chains, but if you have not yet broken them with your mind, you are *still* in captivity.

When the classes were over, we walked in small bands back to our respective homes. There was no peace on our way back home. There were fights all over the road. This group would either fight against that group or kids from one village would fight against kids from a different village.

Other fights erupted as kids scrambled for sugarcane leftovers. Villagers on both sides of the main road sold sugarcane to our school. Buyers would cut the end of the sticks because they were not very sweet, so we would scramble for the leftover ends.

On the fights, my mind can recall a certain scene. One group quarreled with a certain big boy. It started during school so they agreed to deal with him when the classes were over. The gong sounded a knocking-off echo, so they rallied and the path was full. Soon they were on him. They buried him under themselves. He was helpless. They soaked his notebook before ripping it apart. Before they let go of him, they stripped him of his clothes and they forced him to carry them in his hands. It was shameful and girls laughed scornfully. The ringleader said that the big boy was stupid because he refused to say the 'Sorry,

Boss!' of slaves. Yes, this was an apology one could make not to get beaten. You had to speak after the one who was about to beat you. It was a better way of covering your shame, a shame of being beaten before everyone.

I remember one day, it was my turn and I said the `Sorry, Boss!' of slaves to the guy who wanted to beat me before the huge crowd. I had to do it. `Say "Sorry, boss!"' commanded that tough boy. I had accidentally broken his pencil.

`Sorry, Boss,' I repeated after him.

`I am stupid.'

`I am stupid.'

`I eat your feces thinking it's sausage.'

`I eat your feces thinking it's sausage.'

`I drink your urine thinking it's milk tea.'

`I drink your urine thinking it's milk tea.'

After that, I was done and let go without being beaten.

Sometimes I loved it when my mother sent a youth to pick me up with his bike. She gave him a cloth that he laid on a crossbar before I sat down. I mostly sat in a way a woman sits on a bicycle traditionally. I did not sit by letting the crossbar between my legs. At times I could sit right on the carrier but I did not like it because my legs had to be tied to a bar. This was so because my toes could easily get caught in the running tyres as he cycled.

I was very impressed with how he had grown into an expert at his machine. On a hilly place he wholeheartedly applied a force to the pedal with the tip of his toes as he took in a deep breath. Shortly he would release all the air at once through the nose and mouth. When I tried to look back I saw that every single pedal drove us to the next inch. When the road turned sloppy, he relaxed himself. At that point he did not pedal and he breathed at a normal rate. He slightly applied the brakes and my face came in contact with a gentle wind from trees that bordered the dusty road. The gentle wind brought a sense of peace in my mind. It was peace that took me away from those tough boys, those fights and the scorching sun that roasted our bodies every time we knocked off from school. When it was dry in the land, the soil was as hot as hell. As we walked back, we had to walk on the short plants path-side to shield our bare feet from the heat that the soil underneath heartlessly sent to the surface.

At home, before I dropped my notebook, my grandmother would welcome me while smiling. 'You are back from school already,' said she most days. 'Go and check on the earthen pot. I have prepared something for you.' She would instruct me to take the roasted potato or boiled banana or boiled cassava in her cooking hut.

My mother would also welcome me. "You have come,' said she most days while wiping off tears due to smoke as she cooked. `Take off your shoes, uniform, and notebook first before I tell you a good story.' I would do as she demanded. In fact, she had already made her point clear that my shoes were for school only; no shoes when going out to play. `Check in the plate. There is food.' She would then unfold the good story. Most of the food I found was similar to the food I found at my grandmother's house. In fact they mostly shared. My favorite was *mkate*, an African bread. I liked it when it was still hot. It was more delicious with steam and a good smell. It was made from ripe bananas. They were peeled and pounded in a wooden vessel with a pounding stick. After that a good amount of flour was added. The mixture was pounded again. Then the mixture was molded into balls in fresh banana leaves. The balls were thrown into a cooking pot placed on cooking stones with a fire burning in its midst. The mouth of the pot was covered with a fresh banana leaf to trap the evaporating steam. After few minutes, one would eat the balls and accompany the swallow with cold water kept in an earthen pot.

As I ate I would just sit alone in the house. My eldest sisters, Jane and Gertrude, would have just left for school. They were in Secondary School by then. They were going to afternoon classes. To make myself happy, I would climb into one of the compound's guava trees to enjoy a swing from its branch. My grandmother had previously placed a chameleon in it to stop us from swinging. She said we were either going to fall from the tree or break the branch.

As kids, a chameleon was a scary animal. It was widely said that it spit burning charcoal, and once it caught your hair with its fingers, it would never leave you. You were going to die with it on you.

So instead, I liked to browse through history books that were on the worn-out shelf. I did not know how to read by then, so I was just interested in the pictures. Some of the pictures were so attractive. I wished I could read the lines below them to know more about the pictures. There were pictures of great wars.

I was also curious about the pictures that showed slaves chained by their necks. These were Africans. Nearby was a slave-driver carrying a rifle. Today, when I read history on my own and relate to the modern world, I have learnt that: in this world no man is more clever or foolish than the other. Events we experience in daily life happen for a purpose. Tragic events have happened in human history with the aim of teaching mankind lessons for the betterment of this world. Yes, the world once staged slavery, great wars, apartheid and holocausts from which man suffered fatal consequences. Today, mankind lives to avoid sentencing the world to another period of slavery, apartheid and further holocausts and great wars.

When the sun had gone down, we loved to sit together as a family while the *koloboyi* gave the dim light from its burning string soaked in a small tank of paraffin. The flame was unstable from the winds that swept during night time. When one carried the *koloboyi*, the flame had to be cupped with hands to shield it from the wind. By then my mother was said to be cooking. My brothers and sisters loved to sing aloud by heart `Old Macdonald.' It was in one of the books they read in school.

Old Macdonald had a farm,
E-I-E-O!

After our supper and riddles at the family fire, before we slept, my mother tested my brothers on how they were mastering the Apostles' Creed. They were about to be tested on Catholic Church exams. They could recite it aloud by heart. I could hear them, for I slept in the middle as we shared one blanket. I joined their mat when my mother sent me out of her bed because I was wetting her blanket. My brothers grumbled, forced to have me on their mat, but they had no choice. I enjoyed sleeping in the middle, especially on cold nights because as my brothers scrambled for the small blanket, I was always covered. My mother had, many times, cautioned them to be careful or else they were going to completely tear the whole blanket into two halves.

CHAPTER EIGHT

It never rain but pours

The months hatched into a year. It was now 2001 and I got to Standard Two. I had performed well in all three academic terms of Standard One.

Unlike my shoes, I still held onto my plastic bag and the bottle too. Almost all of the kids in our class, and the school at large, were always barefoot. Why did I go barefoot? It might appear foolish to your eyes when I reveal it, but I have to. It made me feel shy to be one of the very few students who put on shoes out of all the barefooted kids in our school. Now that I had spent a year at this school, I understood why the majority of the students were not in shoes on my first day to this school, but also why shoes never brought a new day in the kids' life.

Although I was used to the school and the main path to it, which had now shortened as compared to the first day of school, my mother never stopped cautioning me when the maize was green in the gardens. 'Make sure you walk with your friends, in a group,' said she often. Rumors had gained ground that either certain kids or women had been kidnapped or had their private parts chopped off. This was in a distant land. 'And avoid using shortcuts. No one should ever trick you to follow them. When school is over, just walk straight here. Do you hear?' she would echo emphatically.

I remember one day she beat me severely when I came late from school. I had stopped by at a friend's compound. There was *sadaka*, a traditional feast, honoring a distant ancestor of the compound. Though we ate and ate and ate until our stomach got full to bursting, my mother still laid a hand on me for not coming straight home.

The year was a very bad year in general. My eyes began developing a health problem. I was a child, so I might lie if i claim to know the actual disease of the eyes. I had difficulty seeing at a distance and especially in sunny weather. At home my mother gave me a flat cap to block the sun. The cap was not my size. Even if I had adjusted it at the back, it would not fit my head tightly. This drove my friends to make fun of me all the times I had it on.

But at school, I did not wear it. My Standard Two teachers asked me to sit on a stone close to the front, not because I told them, but because I failed to read a number on the board from where I was sitting. `I should never see you in the back again,' the teacher said. It embarrassed me, though I honestly never knew why. One day, after moving my stone seat to the front, the blackboard fell on me. I felt great pain. As would happen to other classmates, when this happened I was the laughingstock of my class.

Amidst my eye problem, a certain elderly woman invited me to her home. She was from a neighboring compound. She wanted to give me traditional treatment for my disease, but it never worked because of the way I was supposed to conduct it. She advised me to stand outside of the door while it was shut, and she would stand on the other side of the door. She wanted us to articulate certain words in a serious manner.

'Go! Go! Go!' I spoke as I knocked on the door with my folded fingers.

'Yes? Who is it?' she replied.

'Me. I have children in my eyes,' replied I.

'Where are you from?'

'From the eye-disease world.'

This was the nature of the conversation and I found it funny. As a child I laughed frequently, but this innocence betrayed me. Looking at how much I laughed, she advised me to come back another day when I could be more serious.

When I got back to our compound, I began imitating the conversation I had at the medicine woman's compound. The people in our compound laughed, and the more they laughed the more I imitated the conversation. It reached her ears and she said, in capital letters, that she should never see my feet in her compound again.

With each sunrise and sunset, my eyes kept dying. The teacher told me not to go back to school again until my eyes were healed. I was going to infect my fellow learners. Was it because of the yellowish stuff that gathered at the corners of my eyes? The yellowish stuff would completely close my eyes every morning I woke up, and I had to struggle to open them.

So I stayed a week out of school. One day, Jane took me to Zomba Central Hospital. The eye specialist rebuked my sister strongly, so strongly so that I saw in my sister's eyes a sense of regret for bringing me to the hospital. She delayed taking me to the hospital sooner. The specialist made his point clear that my eyes were about to turn blind because their condition was worsening. I was given an injection in my left eye and it was sealed in a white plaster. I was told to go every morning for a check-up. One day, the specialist worked on my eye with a sharp blade. He said he scraped a blister in my eye. It was a very painful process, as I recall. At home I stayed indoors for weeks. I did not play and go to school.

Towards the end of the year, my mother got slightly sick. She could still hoe and cook but not as strongly as before. I was worried.

CHAPTER NINE

The weeping child

I did not turn into a blind boy and my mother did not die from her sickness. I may say 2001 was a good year.

In 2002 and I was now in Standard Three. This was a huge source of pride for the little me. I was no longer to be using a pencil, but a pen. I needed more than one notebook, whole and unsliced. But the most important of all was the shift from the under-tree classroom into a shed classroom. In our day, not an ordinary student could do that.

In fact there was a special trend when it came to classrooms at Mulunguzi Primary School. The idea was to determine 'Who goes into this or that classroom' and 'Who is not supposed to go in this or that classroom.' This was the trend: Standard One and Two, under the tree; Standard Three and Four, in sheds; Standard Five and Six in brick-walled classrooms but with no desks; Standard Seven and Eight, brick-walled classrooms with desks.

As usual, the year opened with villagers busy with garden works, but in that year the sky was not promising for good rain. The rain clouds were not so thick. The scarce rains were not enough for the beans, peas, and maize in the people's gardens. In most gardens, the maize was partly dried and termites often brought down the stalks. In our garden, the crops had weak stalks and they were stunted.

Such rain conditions were a solid source of worry to the people of our land. To them, in fertile soils and good rains lie great wealth. Fertile soils and abundant rains were and still are the center of their world. No wonder elders of old rains, whose hairs had grown gray, every day worried about the unpromising sky.

`The moon has come with a bag,' I heard one elder worrying that there was trouble.

`What this year has for us in store, we cannot tell,' spoke the second elder

`We will see it,' said the first elder. `The thick clouds gather but out of nowhere they just disappear.'

`If this continues, there will be fire this year.'

This was drought. Yes, I heard so. Several times a politician spoke about it from the radio. In my great nation, a thing like drought is a solid subject for a politician to walk with energy to a podium to talk about.

The whole of January, my mother's health was bad. She stopped hoeing and mostly lied on the mat in the sun. This was strange, but I still kept going to school. She was looking different. I saw her eyes disappearing into their sockets. I avoided every look she gave straight into my eyes. I could tell she was in great pain.

One night she cried out in pain, asking to be buried alive. I can effortlessly recall this, as if it had just happened yesterday.

'I would rather die than live,' my mother cried. 'Tell my brother, Austin, to buy a coffin right now and bury me,' she kept on. My eyes were filled to the brim with tears. It was hard for my ears and heart to accommodate the wish of my sweet mother.

'Don't speak like that,' my grandmother came in with a broken hope. 'The boy is crying,' she said after seeing that I was brokenhearted and tears stood in my eyes. But my mother's pain was immense, too great to stop her from wishing she could just die. It was a very tough experience for me. There are no words with which I can explain how rough it was to go through this moment.

On one day, my mother called for me and strangely just looked at me, never saying a word. Was I grown up enough to read people's faces? Her face had shrunk, her eyes deeper in their sockets than before. I felt my young life breaking apart. She had been the center of my world, and I felt this center weakening and weakening.

On February 13th, that's when it happened. The day started as usual. People raised their hopeless eyes in the sky which had no thick rain clouds. They complained. My mother, too, was brought out in the sun. I stayed close by, never thinking about school.

On that day, the sky was perfectly clear. I had heard the oldest man in our compound attaching a meaning to the clearness of the sky. He said it might be a sign of rain later in the day.

I had just started playing hide-and-seek with other kids. Out of nowhere I saw elderly women run into the house where my mother had been taken because the sun had risen in the sky. It caught my attention. The unusual cry from the elderly women sounded a mourning gong, and as quick as a wink, the clear, sunny weather turned mild and windy. A mourning shadow fell across our compound. Funeral winds swept through it repeatedly. The 13th of February is the day I recognize as the worst day of my life. I saw my future becoming dark, darker and darkest.

At the close of that day, the sky was not perfect. There was a faint moon. A mild wind blew, taking with it brave but empty and hopeless cries from our compound. My mother was not going to rise up to life again.

At daybreak, village men took hoes and shovels and dug a grave for my mother. They brought with them a sorghum stalk. They had marked my mother's height on it to guide them as they dug. It brought a sharp pain to my heart, and I felt my heart cracking into tiny, uncountable pieces.

For the first time I hated the soil. It felt like it was no longer the same soil from which we had been getting our yearly yields. It was going to swallow my mother for good. It inspired my poem:

Soil

In you
My mother is sleeping.
Will she wake up?
Will you vomit her out?

Oh no!
Your mouth is sealed from vomiting
But open, for endless swallowing
And filled, you never get.

Still Ma, underneath,
Hear me.
For you, I weep
Sun-up, Sun-down.

A torn motherhood.

Poor woman.

My eyes are heavy

I shed so many tears.

In the afternoon, men carried her and people cried and cried and cried. My tears were not enough to wash away the sweet memories and things she did in my life. There are no words in the world with which I can express how it felt. It was better for me to watch my mother toiling and struggling, trying to flee herself from the powerful hands of poverty on her neck, than to see her lying in that box, lifeless. This was a woman who saw her life dark, darker and darkest. At the edge of the darkest part waited a coffin.

CHAPTER TEN

I hear of a `donor'

Time passed. Life was different now. Our grandmother began taking care of us. We took care of her animals: the goats and pigs. It was not only us, to be honest; all the young lads of the compound did. As lads, to feed the goats and the pigs was like a game to us. We were very much interested in holding the goats by plaited ropes.

With the passing on of my mother, to feed the goat and pigs was no longer an interesting thing. This time around, it was for survival. Today when I see a little boy in the village tying a goat to a peg for fun, I know one day he will not be happy because he will have to tether his goat for survival.

On weekend mornings we liked sitting or standing around a burning fire. We warmed ourselves by burning old stalks. When the burnt ashes were hot, we roasted cassava, maize, and sweet potatoes, but I liked the roasted sweet potatoes most. I liked sweet potatoes that were roasted on a hot clod of earth. The mound of earth was covered with the burning dried leaves of pea plants. The earth would get red hot from the hot ashes. After that, the clod of earth was cracked and the potatoes were covered with the cracked earth.

The roasted crops acted as our breakfast. After eating, we would wash our throats with water. We would brush our teeth with brushes made from small sticks. One end of the sticks was crushed into fine hairs. The old and cold ashes could be spread on the fine hairs and continuously rubbed on our teeth. After some minutes of the brushing the mouth was washed with water.

After roasting, we went into the bush to fetch succulents for the goats. In rainy seasons, green grass was all over in the gardens, so we just tethered them to pegs that had been hammered into the ground in the green grasses.

The pigs were fed with banana stems. The banana stems were cut from bananas that bordered many surrounding gardens. Apart from the banana stems, we also gave them maize husks. Both the husks and banana stems were mixed with salt before being thrown to the pigs. I do not know whether pigs like salt. As kids we saw Austin, a gray-haired man, throwing the salted feeds to the pigs. So in our clan we say: an experienced mother dog does not paw at a hole for nothing.

Then we would either go fishing or hunting mice. When people harvested maize, we liked to dig for mice. Mice were hunted in different ways. We would either set traps or dig them from their holes. The traps were set in their tracks. Groundnuts, cassava, maize grain or roasted maize husks were placed on the trap as bait. The traps were either made from hollowed bamboo or metal tins.

I liked the digging way. We had an old ritual before hunting. Just before you went into the bush, older boys gently rubbed the skin of your head. If it was hard, you were sent back. Hard-skinned heads always brought bad luck, they said. But if the skin of your head was soft, it meant you would bring good luck to the group.

In the bush, only the digger was supposed to poke his finger into the hole. Minus that, the group was going to dig for nothing. The hole was going to collapse, it was said.

When the hole was slanting into the ground, the digger was supposed to strip naked. He fetched a grass stalk and measured the length of his manhood organ on the stalk. The measurement was tied together with a bundle of dried banana leaves. Then the leaves and the stalk were inserted to the hole as the bundle burnt on one end. The digger kept blowing air until the whole bundle was consumed by the fire. It was said that when he resumed digging the hole ceased to head slantingly. I say it was said because I cannot confidently admit that I had ever seen a hole changing direction soon after the smoking. In fact as children, we were not allowed to get close to the hole. Our job was to fetch dried banana leaves, carry hoes and clear the spot where we dug mice. We also searched holes that were possible emergency holes for the mice.

Some days it rained lightly and mild and then the sun rose. On such days, we drew lines with charcoal enclosing some holes at the entrance of our compound. Children from other compounds also did the same. Before the sun shone directly overhead, black-winged ants came from the holes. We called them *Nyamu*. Their stomachs were coloured yellow.

Before dark, small white-winged ants, *Ngumbi,* also flew. I remember we would chase and flap them with our cloths. We put them into containers that had water. The catching of the ants never saw one's age. It ranged from kids, young adults and even the grown-ups. `Yanga iyooo! Yanga iyoooo!' people shouted as they chased and flapped the white-winged ants in the young darkness.

There was one funny thing about the kids when they chased. Most of them were naked. Their manhood organs flapped in a way a fish gently flaps its tail in waters. Of course mine too, had flapped some three or four years ago.

Actually when the rains stopped, they marked game-time for children in many villages. We first enjoyed the sight of *Uta wa Leza,* rainbows. When it got calm, we played and played and played.

In one place, young boys and girls played *chibelemuda*. They drew a circle on the ground. Then two diameters ran through it, cutting it into four equal segments. Two people got into the circle. The pair faced each other while stretching their legs between the diameters that bordered the two semi-circles. Then they began singing:

Eh Chibelemuda!
Changanga!

Eh Chibelemuda!
Changanga!

As they sang, they rotated in all the four segments of the circle in a dancing manner. The rule was, if your partner moved a leg into the left radius, you were also supposed to move yours into the left radius of your semi-circle. But both players used all four radii.

In another place, people played *phada*. Each one had *mwana*, a piece of an earthen pot. They threw them into boxes they drew on the ground. They could play and play and play until the champion cried, "*Jenta jenta!*" and the others cried "*Jenta!*"

Those were the days when the rains had just stopped and the day was calm again.

One day, *anduna*, the messenger of the chief, moved around the village. He was writing down the names of all the orphaned children.

A week later, the Village Crier with his gong and whistle moved around the village at night echoing. He was a young lad from the chief's compound.

'Tomorrow! Tomorrow!' his voice flew in the utter darkness of that night. '*Pyooo! Pyooo!*' That was his whistle. 'Only those children whose names were written down should gather at daybreak at the village ground.' His echo grew more and more distant as he disappeared into the night past our compound. At times when he got on a hilly place your ears could catch the echo from his voice and the gong.

So in the morning people gathered at the *bwalo*, chief's ground. Catherine brought me, my two brothers and sister to the ground. There was a big mango tree whose leaves provided a shadow to the ground. The chief addressed us that there was a certain group of *Azungu*, Whites, that was going to be supporting us, being orphaned kids. I do not know which continent these Whites were from. Maybe from Europe or America, I was not sure.

After a few days we travelled to a distant land. Honestly I do not remember the name of the place, but we headed east. What I recall is the name of the local politician of that place, Mrs. Gillian Mulumbe.

We walked and walked and walked. We did not stop. We walked and walked and walked. Some kids cried on the way because they were either thirsty or their feet hurt. My memory is still fresh; no one was in shoes, including the grown-ups who were escorting us.

At one point we came to an angry river. Its waters made a thundering noise. Our group was terrified. The running waters sent a great fear in my young life. We had to hold each other's hands and form a chain and cross as a group. Today when I recollect this unity and relate to how Malawi, Africa and the world have been divided into rival camps along tribal, religious and racial lines that cannot move ahead as one, I am always disappointed. The betterment and prosperity of our nations, continents and planet depend on our ability to hold hands as one people and face `angry rivers' regardless of the difference in tribe, race and religion. Here little orphans, poverty-, hunger- and thirst-stricken, managed to hold hands and cross an angry river. Unity is strength.

We got to the place. There were a million other dirty, orphaned children. Orphans of many surrounding villages had been invited. The kids were dressed in what I can confidently say were rags. By the way they were dressed, one might think they did it deliberately to impress the White man. But this was their real world.

I saw Mrs. Mulumbe. She was light-skinned and you might think she was one of the Whites. Her light skin plus her neatness added to her beauty.

From her mouth I heard a word which I mastered quickly. Her whole speech was in Chichewa, but this word lacked a Chichewa translation. This word was 'donor.' Our photos were taken. The sound of cameras clicking was everywhere. The photos, we were told, were for our donors.

When we got back to the village, the story of the 'donor' was in the air in most compounds. It was a new word to my people, I am sure. People said many things about the 'donor.' Some said he was a powerful man, possessing greater wealth than any other villager in my village, even in distant ones. Others said he was a man from 'outside' concerned about the welfare of others. Rumors were gaining ground about the 'donor.' I just found it funny how the elders of our compound pronounced the word 'donor.' It sounded like one of the fried food (doughnuts) I had known before, so it was funny.

Many days and nights came and went since our photos were taken. We kept on with school. By then I had managed to get a uniform. One had become small for my brother who was getting taller and taller. The rate at which he was getting taller was as if he was in a race to see who could touch the sky first. However, it was a little too big for me, but my grandmother just told me that it was fine because I was growing up. Someday it would give me a tighter fit.

There was one thing that I noted when someone gave you clothing or shoes beyond your size. You were forced to keep and wear it. You could not give or sell it to someone else. If it was a big shirt, it never survived long enough to fit you properly. The shirt grew threadbare before your height even caught up with its size.

At one point in time, my uncle gave my brother a pair of shoes. They were so much bigger than the size of his feet. He could not sell them or else he was never going to get anything from the uncle again if he was found out. Instead, he became a lender. People within our compound could come and borrow them when they had special occasions.

Yes, I had high expectations for Standard Three, but I later learnt things were not as I expected. The first challenge was penmanship. We had been using pencils in Standard One and Two. So to use a pen for the first time was a challenge. They got slippery when writing. They caused inaccuracy. Their ink also easily flooded over from their tubes.

Second, there was much use of English as the medium for communication. By then I had not even mastered reading Chichewa, my own tongue. The only English statement I had mastered, just like any other kid in our village, was `Hello Uncle Fuvan. Give me sweets.' We often said that to Uncle Fuvan, Mr. Meyer's son. Mr. Meyer was a Whiteman who came from South Africa and the owner of the Meyer's Residence.

Our Standard Three teachers, Mr. Dzimbiri and Mrs. Mwayang'ana, made communication in English a compulsory thing. Even to go outside to answer the call of nature, you were supposed to ask for the permission in English. `Please teacher, may I go out' to some may sound simple to say. This is so because they have either gone high with school or it is their mother tongue. But in those days, it can be equated to the task of climbing the highest mountain you have ever seen or known.

I remember one day I let *it* out right in the classroom. I had tried to practice on my own how I was going to ask the teacher to let me out. `Please may…out,' I murmured to myself. `No. It is not like that,' I was debating inwardly. The next thing I saw was my own trail. It came out with steam. And it was coloured due to urea.

CHAPTER ELEVEN

A new public school, new tough boys

My uncle Austin moved out to the Police Camp residence. He had accepted the offer of a house in town. Previously, he was operating from our village and was riding on his motor-bike to work. Actually, our village was close to the police camp. He decided to take me with him to town. I packed my few clothes and an old blanket in a plastic sack. I also brought along a mat whose reeds were going loose.

Life in town was different from that of my village. I had to forget about the `I exist because we exist' thing. Life in town was about `me' and `my family.'

Although cars passed by the dusty road in the village, there were not as many as those in town. Children here, both younger and older than me, were always clean and well dressed.

After a week, I started school at Police Camp Primary School. The school had a lot of buildings. The painted walls of the buildings were very dirty. Some naughty students had written on the walls, and the walls were always stained. The windows were broken, too. The school had a slogan: "NO GAIN WITHOUT PAIN."

Most of the students were in shoes, high socks, uniforms and carrying backpacks. There was one new thing; children would still wear shoes even when school was over for the day. When they went out to play, they put on their shoes. I say it was a new thing because I grew up believing that shoes were only worn for special occasions, not to playing grounds.

At my new school, there was a rich library. Teachers also distributed books to students and students could keep the books for the whole term. This was a far-fetched dream for a student at my former school. It was at this school where I started to read in English on my own. After school I practiced with the book I was given to keep for the whole term. I mastered reading in Chichewa and English at Standard Three, but I could not speak English on my own.

There were also tough boys at my new school. Police Camp Primary was another tough public school. It was a meeting place for learners from various areas. Some students came from areas of bad records due to high crime rate and prostitution. There were learners from the ghettos of Chikanda, Mpondabwino, Chizaro and Fokolande. Any native of Zomba is aware that these have the worst slums and squatters in the region. The larger part of the students was children of police officers.

But most of the tough students were from the ghetto. If you looked at them, they were always dirty. Their shoes had holes by their big toes and their clothes were threadbare. They were involved in deadly fighting. At break times they would go to the Police cafeteria and scramble for the food leftovers. If you bought a piece of food during break, you had to grip it tight in your hands. They would either snatch it from you and run or hit your hand to drop it to the ground. Those were hard days. In class they liked to tie together the uniform laces that were on girls' uniforms. They would secretly tie together more than two girls. When these girls rose up, they would find that they were tied together, and it was embarrassing.

If you had a pen, you had to insert a sticker in it with your name on it. These unkempt boys were 'young thieves in a formal school.'

There was one tough boy who, as long as I live, I will never forget what he did to me. His name was Simeon. He was the son of a police officer living at the Band Line. He forced me and my friend, Trouble, to buy freedom from him to attend classes. He either demanded food or money or else you were going to learn from the window while outside. He was a hard-hearted boy and for the first time I wished I could go back to my village.

'*Phwanga dollar yaine,*' was his greeting. He demanded money from us each morning. I remember one day I tried to lie to him, saying that I had no money. He searched me thoroughly at the toilets. He discovered a coin that I had carefully hid inside my shorts. I had cleverly made a pocket inside my shorts to insert my coins to hide them from the lion. He became as violent as a volcano.

'*Phwanga ukunditenga ngati kape?*' he roared wanting to know whether I thought he was a stupid boy. 'We will see.' This was a three word statement but there was a lot of meaning in it especially when it came to boys of Simeon's category. My mind can effortlessly recall an earlier moment when a naughty boy said the same three words just before stripping my pair of shorts in front of girls. I had refused to share with him my food during a recess. He hit my hand so that I would drop it to the ground but he was unsuccessful. I gripped my food tightly as if I had a magnet hand. It angered him and he said 'We will see.'

He waited until I was about to walk past a group of girls of one classroom. He walked behind me silently, on tip-toes as if a cat which was about to pounce on a busy rat, and brought my shorts to the ankles. I was caught unexpectedly. The girls fell into laughter. As quick as a flashlight, I pulled my shorts back to the abdomen. In my soul it was not as quick as it was. The heart of my soul fell apart seeing the girls having fan at my manhood privacy exposed.

My pair of shorts was not threadbare so my manhood privacy was covered and I wore dignity. Here a heartless boy stripped me of my dignity. Only the heavens know that I single it out as one of the moments I have felt most empty about myself. The privacy that was exposed was the same that I had exposed when I put on threadbare shorts in the village. Here it carried weight because I was mocked and pushed into it.

I never chose poverty. All those childhood years I knew there was no dignity in putting on threadbare shorts and I lived as I hoped for a brighter day. In our societies, people put effort into taking their lives to a new day. So if our neighbor is making effort to come out of the struggle, and we mockingly push them back into the struggle, we strip them of their dignity and drive them hopeless. It is only when we have set a ladder for them to step out of the struggle they feel determined to go forward.

Before the final bell rang on the day Simeon had scared me, I staggered towards the teachers. I made up an illness and ran home. This was maybe to search for more coins to cover my `offence' when tomorrow came. The funny thing was, when I went home I picked up with life as if nothing happened at school.

Simeon had his own naughty crew in class. At times their group held your feet and raised your legs up. After that they would hold you in front of everybody, including girls. It was embarrassing. As you struggled to free your legs, the big shorts we had put on nearly exposed our private parts. Our days in school were hard days.

I clearly remember (it is hard for me to share but I have to): one day a member of his crew forced some dirty wound onto my lips. I had looked at his wound as it discharged some pus, and that was an offence to him.

'Do you want to eat it?' he began. I just smiled for I thought he just joked. He touched his finger to the dirty wound on his big toe. Then he extended it onto my lower lip. It landed and I felt it. Oh no. God! I was very furious and he got scared. I was on my feet to go outside to look for a stone to crack his head, but I quickly went against it. I did not want to repeat my previous mistake. Yes, my previous mistake. I had cracked my neighbor's head before. His name was William, the son of a police officer. I brought him down to a hard floor in a fight. There was blood all over and I was scared and I regretted it.

So instead I reported the matter to the teacher. That was my newly found courage. It turned Simeon into a frightened boy, for one day it was going to be him. The teacher rebuked him in front of the class. At the end he removed a few huge stumps within the school. My heart cooled down.

After school I liked to play with other kids. There were Blessings, Diana, Chifuniro, Henry, Wille, Ndiuzayani and Chikaiko. With them we played many games. We also liked to play with clay soil that we dug from a distant water-logged creek. With it we made cars and humans of our choice.

As children we loved to listen to the Police Band playing on their musical instruments. In those days there were some famous tunes I loved to listen to. They were played by the Police Band. They played *King Cotton, College March, Lost Beef of England, March through Georgia* and others. It was all great.

I also had a good friendship with the grown-up Dicky Ilinga, Ndiuzayani's older brother. We were so close. When I brought some fruits from my village, I shared some with him. He liked the fruits, especially when he was fasting in the months of Ramadan. He was Muslim.

When I was not outside, I was inside watching TV. I remember my first time watching TV. It was so funny. A car at high speed had zoomed toward the screen, and I thought it was going to run over me. I sprang out of my chair and everyone laughed. That was the same thing one might also think when watching soccer. The camera would focus on the ball as it rolled. One might decide to catch it only to realize that it was still in the TV.

Anyway, everything has its beginning. I was not the only one. I also heard about a certain village boy who tried to keep a song for his uncle when it played on a radio. This boy's Uncle liked a certain song and the boy knew it. One day it was played on the radio but the uncle was away to work. The boy recognized the song, and knowing how it makes his uncle happy, he decided to keep it for him. How? Before the song ended he turned the radio off. He thought the remaining part would resume as soon as he turned it on when the uncle came. When his uncle came home, he excitedly told him that he had his favourite song in store. The boy turned the radio on, only to realize there was a different program on, not the song. The uncle just laughed. This was the story I heard. I do not know whether it really happened or if it was made up.

In those days we watched many things happening around the world. The Iraq War was common on the TV. The Americans were fighting against Saddam Hussein. I recall that as kids we imitated the white soldiers with our play guns. We made our guns with clay or hollowed papaya stalks that were fresh. One group of boys would be named either Vietnamese or Iraq army. The other group was the American army.

This was also the period I saw Osama Bin Laden. He was also commonly broadcast on the screen. Even the Twin Towers coming down, we watched. We watched a plane as it pierced the tip of a very tall building. Then the spot was engulfed in a cloud of dust.

CHAPTER TWELVE

Back to my roots

Years passed. On Fridays I headed to the village where I would spend some of my weekends. Every time I went back to the village, it brought back old memories from before I went to town. I missed many things about the village.

I missed Old Kambalame. He was a man in his sixties or seventies who joined our compound a month before I left for town. He came to work for my grandmother. He cleared and tilled her gardens after harvesting. On his part, he was searching for greener pasture due to a fierce famine that hit Malawi around the 2000s.

I liked his funny stories and I found it hard to leave any place he worked or sat. He was a man of so many stories. Yes, one day he told me that he had killed a lion with his bare hands. He wrestled and wrestled with it. There was a cloud of dust as he wrestled. He removed its tail before he broke its neck. I have not made up this story, but that's what he told. I found such stories good and enjoyable.

I remember one thing that Old Kambalame told about this life. It rings in my ears daily. "Do not be weak in life," he said as he smoked his local tobacco. "A man like you should make things happen."

Similar to him was Chimwemwe, the sweet talker. He was a man of many stories, but he told us one story that was very harmful to a young mind. This was the story. Long, long time ago, a White man, a Black man, a China man, and an Indian man made a long trip to where God lived. God asked them, "What can I do for each of you? Each man was supposed to reply on his own, and get what he asked for.

'What can I do for each of you?' God asked.

White man: "I want you to give me wisdom."

China man: "I want you to give me manufacturing skills."

Indian man: "I want you to give me the knowledge of trade."

Blackman: "...?"

He told us that the ancestor of black people was a shy and sleepy man and was unable to ask for a blessing from God. He often fell asleep soundly as the others made their requests. Time and again the others had to shake him to wake up. So he lost favour in the eyes of God and He cursed the black ancestor and his descendants that they would be poverty stricken in their lives. That was a reason why black people stretched out their hands to beg every time they met whites, Chinese and Indians.

Today, when I recollect this childhood story, I realize that he tried to breed an exaggerated story of poverty in our young minds. I grew up at the very heart of poverty and I have learnt that poverty in man's life is created either through irresponsibility of himself or greed. Out of the two, greed should be singled out as the major cause of almost all poverty in man's life.

Largely, man's poverty is created by other men. God did not create poverty in man's life, but man has developed a strong muscle from greed, used to push another man down to the bottom of the ladder. At the top, he has developed all mechanisms to keep others stuck at the bottom, so the rich get richer and richer and the poor get poorer and poorer. The danger is when another 'Chimwemwe' exists to enslave the mind of the people at the bottom of the ladder with the exaggerated story of poverty from God. And they live in ignorance until their death-knell sounds.

Personally, I believe being rich or poor is the state of the mind and the heart. A man whose mind and heart hold that he is poor will portray in his actions the poverty held in his mind and heart. It does not only take one wearing a torn cloth or sleeping on an empty stomach or walking barefoot to qualify as poor. Even the queen or king in a majestic gown can be poor. Have we not seen or read about a queen or king, in a majestic gown, their conscious going as low as stealing poor people's treasure? Their poverty is internal and usually portrayed through the actions.

So to fight poverty in our societies, we have to start fighting it right in our minds and hearts. The solution to poverty in our societies lies right inside our very minds and hearts. The outside is just there to set a stepping stone. Today, Africa and many other Third World countries are still yoked in poverty since the attainment of independence because an opportunity that is laid by the First World or any well-wisher is mistaken for a solution.

During those years, the `donor' gave us some items. The name of their organization was Global Aids Interfaith Alliance (GAIA). Two or three times, they gave each of us cooking oil, clothes, blankets, *Likuni* (nutritious porridge flour), soap and beans. However, towards 2004, GAIA stopped its support for orphans.

In 2004 I spent my third-term holiday in the village. During the holiday, my head had been impregnated with an idea of remaining in the village for good. I wanted to go back to Mulunguzi Primary School. I had been nursing this idea until it became established.

In fact I loved to amuse other kids with the new games and jokes I had learnt in town. It made me look like a hero to them. When it was a holiday, sons and daughters of our village would come back from distant trading towns. As a kid I brought with me new town things. I taught my friends how to make kites and parachutes with plastic papers. The kites were made with grass stalks. A long suck-string was tied to it. And we held the other end and flew them as planes.

    To make a parachute, we tied a few strings on the edge of the plastic paper. All the strings were extended to a center where they were tied to a small stone. As children we ran after it until it dropped to the ground. So the kites and parachutes were everywhere in our compound and others around. This town knowledge made me famous in our compound and surrounding compounds. I was so famous.

THE ROOTS: A rich soil, a rich people. The ancestors of Prophet Dauda in their compound: (from left to right) Abiti Magana (the great Grandmother), Auntie Catherine, Nganga, Ethel, Dymon. The story starts from this compound.

LONG AT LAST: Proph in late 1999 with sister Jane. The much awaited day. Sister Jane promised to take a photo with Proph. He many times asked her when the photographer would come to the village. The day he appeared wasn't a good one, Proph had just sustained an injury on his thumb. Godfrey accidentally cut him with a hoe while hoeing. Still he had to wipe off tears, tie the thumb with a piece of cloth, and put on his best clothes. He tried as much as he could to portray the best smile and good body language.

`A people from the land of snow': Proph poses with the Mulvanes from Ohio (2008

With Kelly Hagelberg teaching basic science to reform school boys

The team retreat at Tasty Bites after missionary works in the surrounding villages

With Nathan Jeffers, making a film for the Passion Center in 2013

As a secondary school teacher intern in 2016

Light at the end of the tunnel: graduation day in 2016

Part Two

The Clearing Sky

At some point people find themselves on a battlefield. And they might be willing to fight. But how each one of them stages the fight determines the winner and loser. All of us orphaned kids were on a battlefield of poverty. A kid who fought with a dream and vision came out a winner. I grew up in a home where poverty ate up all the opportunities and it has been a mother-teacher to me, so that when the generous throws an opportunity in my path, I grab it like a hungry dog and take full advantage of it with a focus on my destiny.

CHAPTER THIRTEEN

A blessing in disguise!

Yes, I restarted school at Mulunguzi Primary School. It was hard to adjust to my old school after I had missed it for some years. No buildings had been added. The sheds and stones under the mango trees were permanently there. Just as I had left it before, only a few students managed to get the school uniform.

At home, life was hard, too. Catherine had died a year or two ago leaving behind five children. So Catherine's children and us fell under the care of my grandmother.

While in town, I was used to eating breakfast when going to school. But back in the village, it was different. No breakfast.

I can assure you when going to school I carried a notebook and a pen because the Malawi government of our day distributed free notebooks and pens and pencils in school. I do not know whether the modern government continues with it.

When coming home from school, one was not sure whether he or she was going to find lunch. The wise, as I was, was supposed to make his stomach not expect a meal. I trained myself to make my stomach neutral: I was going to eat or not.

As soon as I reached home I would walk straight to the cooking hut and check the cooking stones. If they had been covered with fresh cooking flour I would activate my stomach for lunch. The fresh flour indicated that *nsima*, thick porridge, had been recently cooked. If not covered with flour, I maintained the no-food state. At times I found food, though the cooking stones were not covered in flour. It was possible grandmother had cooked *Futali*. This was sliced cassava cooked with groundnuts powder. It was one of my favourite.

By then my sisters Jane and Gertrude had graduated from Secondary School. They secured very low-paying jobs in town. Jane worked in a Chinese shop while Getrude worked in a telephone shop.

I remember on one payday Jane bought me a Chinese suit: shorts, and a T- shirt labeled PUMA. The shorts became my second reliable pair for school. The old ones had begun losing their threads, but they had stood the test of time since Julio's mother gave them to me. She was from Chiona's residence. She gave them to me one day after I had helped them harvest maize.

There was one embarrassing thing that happened with the new shorts. They were so soft so that if one did not have underwear on, the tip of the man-hood organ would reach the edge of the short. The tip moved right and left every time one walked. That was what happened with me. Every time I walked around, teachers looked on a bump that had formed in my soft shorts.

A few days following that, all the male students were gathered in one place. It was an all-male assembly. 'Some of you are not putting on your underwear!' shouted the angry teacher. 'You are embarrassing us, fellow males.' From then I decided to put on two shorts. The soft one acted as my underwear.

A week or two later, a certain teacher, Mrs. E Ntaukira invited me over. She had a deep friendship with my brother, Godfrey. By then Godfrey was in Standard Eight. She loved him because of his good performance in class and she paid for his part time classes. At her house she gave me some clothing. I was very grateful for that. My memory is as fresh as if it just happened yesterday; she gave me two sets of trousers, shorts and tops. In this life those who help you are not only your blood relatives. The Creator purposely planted some people in our midst, not connected to us in any way, but they have an effect in our life. Sometimes it makes me say that any human who does not affect anyone next to him or her in one way or another lives for nothing.

Mrs. E Ntaukira was another woman whose generosity left a mark on my life. She was a woman who lighted my path of life when darkness fell on it. She paved the way for me into Pastor Eric's orphanage program. Pastor Eric was and is one of the most influential mentors in my life since I got into the orphanage. Where the world saw a hopeless orphan chained in poverty, he saw a kid with potential to succeed through God and education as ladders. I will talk about Eric and his orphanage program later for it is where the *man* in me was raised.

A new thing had sprouted at Mulunguzi Primary School. I used to sit by the window in class. Every time I stood up, I saw a grown man playing soccer with some dirty kids. He also played jump rope with the kids. This often aroused curiosity in my head. At his age, he was not supposed to play children's games. At the village level, he was supposed to be a man who would rule a compound and bring honor to it. He should be a man of honor with extraordinary manly achievements in the land, rather than just playing tagging games, soccer and jump rope with the children.

Every time we left school for the day, I could see children taking meals in a grass-thatched house. It had dirty walls. Its mud walls were splashed with raindrops and it was standing in a bending position. Two or three times, I wondered whether the dirty house was going to fall on the kids as they ate inside.

One of the kids in the dirty house was the clever Phuzo. One day as we played our usual game of who could send his urine high than the other, I asked him a question.

'What do you do in the ruin?' I wanted to know.

'We eat, sing and pray,' he replied briefly.

'Why you?'

'I don't have a father and a mother,' replied he while laughing though I saw a slight expression of embarrassment on his face. I could not tell why.

'So what?' I bravely tried to switch to make him laugh for the personal questions wrote the embarrassment on his face. He laughed.

CHAPTER FOURTEEN

My adoption: I join the house

Before the academic year came to an end, I found myself in the dirty house too. I was in the second group to join the house. Later on, my American friends fondly called this group the Second Phase. Mrs. E Ntaukira, the matron at the time, identified the needy students from the school to join the feeding house. So I joined.

The first week was a tough week. We had to adjust. One thing I noted was that the kids at the feeding house lived as a *family*. We were brothers and sisters.

The man who I used to see playing with the children moved around and greeted us warmly. His name was Mr. Pilira Chibwana. The kids fondly called him Uncle Pilira. There was also a guitarist, Mr. Joseph Kumwembe. And the kids called him Uncle Joe.

'Hello,' said Pilira one day.

'Hello,' I answered shyly while holding my notebooks in a plastic sack.

'What is your name?'

'Prophet Dauda.'

'Do you prophecy?' he asked without expecting an answer. In fact, that was the question I was most asked by people I met for the first time.

'No, it is just a name,' I replied.

'What about the name Bongo?' he asked with a fond smile on his mouth. He massaged my shoulders softly. He had a small chip in his front lower teeth. The chip made him speak with a lisp, making him a more sweet man. I liked him so much.

'It is a name I am called at home. But in school I am known by Prophet,' I said while laughing. Other kids who were around also broke out laughing. In fact, in my village I was widely known as Bongo. So some playmates would still call me by that name at school. Within the first week it was also known at the feeding center. Actually, I was given the name by an uncle. He was a drunkard. When he went drinking he liked the music by Kanda Bongomani, a musician from Zaire. I was born when this musician was at his peak, so he nicknamed me after him.

'What standard are you in?' he also asked.

'I am in Standard Seven.'

That was the nature of conversation in the early days at the feeding house. When we were about to take our portions, one kid would shout 'Kusamba M'manja!' It was time to wash our hands. A kid or two would pour water onto our hands from some plastic cups. They took the water from a bucket that was placed nearby.

After cleaning our hands, the women who cooked for us would ask one kid to shower a blessing on the food. These women were from the surrounding villages. And we fondly called them Aunts. There was Auntie Nyerere and Sphiwe's mother.

After eating, Uncle Joe played on his guitar. We sang gospel songs and he shared the Word of God. Many times Uncle Joe and Uncle Pilira talked about *Yesu Khristu*. Of course I had heard about that name before, but not as seriously as at this place. Every single minute kids shouted *Yesu! Yesu!*

There was this popular verse that the kids recited by heart, and their recitation went with hand motions. This was the verse:

'Revelation 3 verse 20!' the leader of the kids would shout. 'Behold I stand at the door and knock: if any man hears my voice and opens the door, I will come in to him, and will sup with him, and he with me.' Those were the kids reciting uniformly.

It was great to see how the kids recited from memory and demonstrated the hand motions. The hand motions were in line with each part of the verse. Every time they recited the verse, the oxygen in the house was charged with excitement.

Having finished with the prayers, we retired back to our respective compounds. On the way we did not fight for sugarcane leftovers. We were already full in our stomachs, and we were taught that *Yesu's* children must not fight.

Actually many things changed since I joined the feeding house. *Kothopola* was an old story. Let me share with you about *Kothopola*. This was a name we used to refer to scavenging. We coined the name to stop our guardians from knowing that we were scavengers. As boys we knew it among ourselves, so we would go in trash cans to search for plastic sacks to make soccer balls. If we found any nice thing, we grabbed it. Sometimes we were tempted to pick out food leftovers dumped in the cans. Most of the times we scavenged from the Chancellor College trash cans.

There was no peace at the scavenging sites. There were fights among groups of scavenging kids. Chikanda boys were a violent group. At times there were conflicts between the boys and either the guards or cleaners. I remember on one day we came to an open ground. It was a very clean place. We saw a white child riding a bike. We wanted to get closer and watch him.

'*Kamwana ka mzungu,*' someone among us whispered that there was a White man's child.

'He is riding a bike,' another boy spoke. We walked towards him with our plastic sacks dangling in our hands.

'What are you doing here?' an angry voice came out of nowhere. It was a security guard. 'There is a white kid here. What do you want to do with him?' he roared.

We did not want to harm him. But we were just curious and excited about it. It was a very rare thing to us to see such a ki grown into an expert with his bike. I do not know whether our dirty appearance qualified us to be harmful. I wonder if sometimes our world has employed the security guard's perspective every time the poor tries to get closer to the rich. In fact, growing up as a 'Have not' taught me one thing: when you are a 'have not', you are mostly viewed as an obstacle to the 'haves.'

He chased us with his whipping stick. I fell into a deep pit as I ran. Even today I fail to understand how I brought myself out from the deep pit to resume running before the guard came to the mouth of the pit.

CHAPTER FIFTEEN

My adoption: This is the Passion Center for Children

Many days went by. Each morning we would go and have our breakfast before school started. After classes we went again for lunch. One day after lunch, Uncle Pilira gathered us as usual. But this was a special day, I could tell. Yes, a prayer was said. We sang our usual songs they had just taught us.

King of Kings
And Lord of Lords
Glory!! Alleluyah!

Jesus Prince of Peace
Glory! Alleluyah!

The way we sang this song was exciting. At first we sang it at the normal speed, then increased the speed a little bit on the second time. The more we sang it, the more the speed rate increased. It was so exciting.

What about that jumping song? This one I loved so much. Uncle Pilira and Uncle Joe stood in front. While we made a single line facing them, we touched our hands to our waists.

> *Peace, love and Joy!!*
> *Jesus!! Jesus!!*
> *Joy!!!*

As we sang we jumped left and right imitating the two men in front.

After the dancing, calmness was restored in the house and we were settled. 'Today I want to tell you about this place,' he began with energy. I could not really tell whether he was doing it for the sake of us, the Second Phase, or if it was going to be the first time for all of us at the house. 'The name of this place is the Passion Center for Children. Passion stands for love. Love of Christ for us.'

His short but bold speech flashed out something in our minds. Before the speech, we just took the Passion Center as the place to eat. When someone on the way or in our villages asked us, 'Where are you going or coming from?' the answer was 'I am going to or I am coming from the eating house.'

At the Passion Center, they also talked about education and life after school. It was all new to me. Until I got to the Passion Center, I went to school because most kids of our village and other villages did. I had remained blind to the secret of school for years and years.

'What do you want to become in the future, after school?' This question became so common at the Passion Center. Some kids said they wanted to become engineers, lawyers, soldiers and policemen. Most of the girls mentioned becoming nurses. 'Then work hard in science subjects and English,' those who wanted to become nurses were told.

Honestly, I thank the heavens he did not ask me personally earlier. I would have had nothing to reply with. I had never thought of a career, as I have pointed out before. In his lengthy speeches about career, Uncle Joe would name the few colleges our country had. One college sounded familiar in my ears. It was Chancellor College. A thought went in my mind when the school sounded familiar *Chancellor College is a place to get education only, not scavenging.*

'The future of your villages lies in the hands of educated people. And you are the future of your villages', he would continue. 'Aim high to go to college and realize your skills to become potential members of our great nation. There will be a time for Malawi to move forward and it will have to be run by educated people. And those educated people will be none other than yourselves,' he empowered and prophesied.

At times, Uncle Joe moved around the villages, visiting our guardians. One day, he was in our compound. From our compound, out of many kids, only Alice and I were part of the Passion Center program.

'The rains were enough this year. And soil brought forth enough,' spoke Uncle Joe to my grandmother before they exchanged greetings and enquired after the health of the people in our compound. She was shelling some maize in a flat round basket.

'Yes. There was moisture in the soil this year. Our only cry was on the salt to apply to the soil,' replied she. By salt she meant inorganic fertilizer.

'Half a bread is better than none. Out of mercies we see the next sunrise,' said he.

'But we should be thankful to the Most High. You can see my granaries are full,' she said while pointing at the two big bamboo granaries that stood at a distance.

'Yes. But how are you staying with the kids? How is life for them since you started taking care for them?' That was where his whole point lay. The sweeping question carried the chief reason why he had visited our compound.

So they talked and talked and talked. At the end of the day, Alice and I had our photos taken.

Before dusk, he left as he chewed some salted groundnuts that my grandmother roasted for him.

CHAPTER SIXTEEN

My adoption: I meet Pastor Eric's Team

Most of the Second Phase kids were barefooted. The First Phase had their shoes, sneakers, and they always shone.

I remember, Pilira used to ask about our shoe sizes. The question may sound simple to those who started wearing shoes at a tender age. Most children in our phase had difficulties providing an answer to this question. Not because they didn't care, but how could they know a shoe size when they seldom found them on their feet? Some had never had shoes on since they were born.

'What is your shoe size?' he asked me one day.

'I do not know. It has been ages since I last had shoes,' I was as flat as the floor. He just moved his head in a sign of understanding.

Each day he kept on asking me. He expected I was going to inquire from my brothers or my sisters. He was right, but they were not sure about it either.

A building that had been under construction was finished. The Passion Center bought a piece of land and erected a Multipurpose

Room with a kitchen on the other end. In the room was where we were going to be conducting prayers and sit as we ate.

It had a special ceremony to open it. Chiefs from surrounding villages, our guardians and other officials were invited. We were all dressed in our clean school uniforms and shoes. I often bent down to re-tie my shoelaces that got loosened every time I tried to walk. You might understand how stupid shoelaces of a new shoe behave. Every time you walk, they loosen.

At the ceremony, we sang a song we had been practicing. It was about how we were grateful for the building. We also asked the chiefs and villagers to be patriotic to this new development. This was the song:

Ife anafe!
Talandira nyumbayi
Titi zikomo kwambiri!!

Tipempha mafumu
Ndi anthu anu
Mutisamalire nyumbayi

After that, we ate and ate and ate until our jaws ached with chewing. Indeed we celebrated for the new house.

It might have been June or July when we were told that some White people, *Azungu*, were coming to the Passion Center. The surrounding area was cleaned in preparation for the visitors. The visitors were from the United States of America. The rumor also spread that they were the founders of the Passion Center for Children.

The day came and it was Saturday. We came earlier and had our breakfast. We got settled and our eyes were fixed to the main dusty road. As soon as the two minibuses drove past a sharp bend, which was at a distance, excitement filled the place. The two minibuses were bringing the white people.

`*Azungu! Azungu! Azungu!*,' as children we shouted getting closer to the cars. The Whites were excited in the cars and the cameras clicked as they smiled.

We sang for them and the clicking of cameras continued. An African child smiled at every click. You might even create a picture in your mind if you have ever seen how people from the West behave with their cameras when they get to a new place. The visitors could even take a picture of a chicken that passed by.

We shook hands with them. This counted as a first time for my black skin to come in contact with white skin.

It was also my first time to clear up a misconception. This misconception had stuck in our heads for many ages. Until I met these Whites, I believed it was just a made-up story. Let me share with you the made-up story I grew up believing: In those days if you asked a kid what he or she knew best about Whites, they would simply tell you that white people eat human beings, especially black people. At times in our village, we were warned to be watchful every time Uncle Fuvan got closer. We were also warned never to jump into any White person's car or accept his gift.

Their leader was Pastor Eric Von Barnau Sythoff. He was a gentleman and tall in height. He had a medium thickness with his head partly grey-haired. He usually wore his sun-glasses, but appeared calm and observant. Most of the times, he stood with Pilira at a distance from where we played. I did not interact with him in the early days. But I did later.

'Hey, man. What's up man?' he spoke as he picked me up. He spoke so fast. I just smiled. By then I had not mastered speaking English, but I was able to unlock the meaning of every statement that came from the visitors. To decode was easy, but to encode was not easy.

'What is your name?' he asked, putting me back on my feet on the ground.

'My name is Prophet Dauda,' replied I, with energy looking at him. Pilira also spoke.

From the feedback on Eric's face, I could tell it was some supplemental information about me.

'What standard are you in?' Eric wanted to know.

'I am in Standard seven.'

'Good Job. Good job.' This was the common word that the visitors used to praise anything impressive that came from us.

On Eric's team, there was Amanda Hearle, Michelle, my buddy John Dixon, Sarah Block, Gaby Canalizo, Weston Martin, Sheila, Misse Mbongo, Don, Matthew Graham, Lee, Jim, and another Matthew. We played different games with them. One funny game was 'Duck, Duck, Goose.' They told us that this is one of the games that kids liked to play in California, where they were from.

We made a circle. One person, either black or white, stood and touched three people. 'Duck duck duck goose!' The one who was touched at the mention of the goose was supposed to start chasing the one standing. The one standing aimed at running faster to sit on the place of the person he touched on the mention of the goose. If the runner got tagged before getting to the place, he or she was supposed to start all over again. But if he or she sat without being tagged, it was the turn of the chaser to say 'Duck duck duck goose' on another person.

They also taught us some songs.

We love the lord!
Yes we love the Lord!!
We love the Lord!!
Yes we love the Lord
Ayee!!! Ayee!!!

To this we would dance and dance and dance until the huge ball of dust, as if an erupting volcano, was formed on the ground.

When I was not dancing, I was with John. He was 19.

'I am from California, thousands and thousands of miles away from Malawi,' said he to me on one day. 'Do you know where America is, on the map?'

'No,' replied I.

'Come inside,' said he while going inside the Multipurpose Room where the *Azungu* had displayed a global map.

'Here,' he pointed the North American landmass. 'We crossed the Atlantic Ocean, then to London, then to Johannesburg, and then finally into Malawi. It was a fifteen hour flight non-stop across the Atlantic Ocean.' I listened to him as he spoke.

'There are mountains, valleys, deserts in California. If you come you will love to walk on the beaches in your sun-glasses. Kids like you like having their sun-glasses on as they are on the beach.' He was also a joker.

John was also interested in knowing about my future plans. 'Bro, what do you want to become after school?' he inquired.

'I want to become a pilot,' said I. In fact, many kids had been talking about Pastor Eric. He was a pilot and I was influenced.

'Nice. Will you fly me?' asked he, extending a hand and expecting a handshake.

'Yes'

'Work hard in Mathematics and Geography and other science subjects. And English, too. English will help you communicate with the Azungus you will be flying on the planes.'

In our interaction, I also gave him Chichewa lessons. I translated a few basic statements in our tongue.

'What is your name?'

'*Dzina lako ndani?*'

'Where do you come from?'

'*Umachokera kuti?*'

'How old are you?

'*Uli ndi zaka zingati?*'

'What standard are you in?'

'*Uli sitandade chani?*'

CHAPTER SEVENTEEN

My adoption: the Missionaries of a Great Slogan

The first week I spent with the Americans was enough to nickname them as the Whites of a Great Slogan: "CARING FOR THE WHOLE CHILD, FOR THE WHOLE LIFE, IN THE WHOLE COMMUNITY."

The following week, many things took place at the Passion Center and Mulunguzi Primary School. New things were brought by the Americans. In fact, since the birth of the orphanage many things had happened in the land. It was through the same orphanage program that the feet of many kids wore new shoes, our hungry stomachs were fed and more importantly we learnt the word of God. Our guardians too, and other villagers were also taught the word of God and empowered in their social lives through a weekly home visitation program. What my clan people say is true: The stranger is the one who carries along a sharp razor (The stranger might have the unexpected solution to great difficulties).

On Monday afternoon of that week, the Whites held a Vacation Bible School (VBS) with us. They worked in teams. Each team had its own activity.

There were teams for singing, dancing, Bible stories, craft-making and games. I very much liked the singing team. This team was comprised of Misse Mbongo, Sarah Block, and Michelle. They stood in front of our class.

'Hello, guys. My name is Sarah Block and she is Misse Mbongo. She is Michelle. We are from the United States of America. We are so excited to be here. Today we're gonna teach you a song. As you sing, you have to demonstrate a hand motion in line with the song,' she spoke through the faithful translator whose name I honestly can't remember. 'This song is liked by kids at your age back in California, the state where I am from.'

Tom tom talalara!!!
Tom tom talaa!!!

Tom tom Talalara!!!
Tom tom Talaa!!!

Toom tooom!!!!!!

It was funny how we sang it with the hand motions. At times we touched our noses. We sang it in the way we sang the King of Kings song.

After Sarah's team came Sheila's team with a Bible story. It was about men of great faith who brought a sick man to Jesus. The men of faith let the sick man through the roof of the houses Jesus was preaching in. 'These men had great faith,' said Sheila when she was winding up the story telling. 'So as children of God, you must have faith in Him just as these men.'

At last we coloured a picture that showed the men of faith bringing the sick man down to Jesus. Her team: Weston, Gaby and Lee, passed out the crayons. We coloured and coloured and coloured with the crayons.

On a day when there was no VBS, the front of the Multipurpose Room was filled to the brim with kids. The kids were as many as the sand. Some were from near villages while others were from very distant villages. I am sure news of the arrival of the White man at the Passion Center spread even to distant lands like wildfire in the dry bush.

Every kid was as busy as a bee, and so were the Whites. In one place a few Whites conducted interviews with the Passion kids. In another place, some Whites taught the kids how to dance and sing.

In our place, we threw a Frisbee to each other. 'This is how we hold it as we throw,' said John while demonstrating to us. We had tried before but we were not perfect. It either got blown away by the wind or went in the wrong direction.

'You wanna give it another try?' he said, handing it to Yamikani, another Passion kid. He threw.

'Not bad,' said Matthew.

'Try to hold it in the edge and throw.' That was Don. This time it moved perfectly to the next kid. 'Good job,' shouted Matthew with excitement.

My turn came to be interviewed. The information obtained was for our American families, our sponsors. We were told that each kid had a family in America. These families also prayed for us all the time. My recall is as clear as in a picture; there were Amanda Hearle and Gaby Canalizo on the interview site. 'Prophet now!' shouted Amanda while writing my name in full on a small whiteboard. She used an erasable marker. I went to where Gaby and the translator were sitting. The translator was Johnstone Dzimkambani, fondly called Uncle Titi.

'What is your date of birth?'

'30th July, 1994.'

'What village are you from?'

'I come from Thom-Allan village.'

'What standard are you in'

'I am in standard Seven.'

'What is your favourite subject?'

'My favourite subject is English.'

'What do you want to become in life?'

'I want to become a Pilot.'

'What is your favourite verse in the Bible?'

'My favourite verse is Ephesus 6:1.'

'What is your favourite colour?'

'My favourite colour is gray.'

'Nice. Go to where Amanda is and have your photo taken,' Gaby winded up. 'Hey Amanda, here comes a Pilot!' said she with excitement. I just smiled.

Before they flew back to Johannesburg, then back to London, then back to Washington DC, they took us up the Zomba Plateau. This is where they were lodging.

I can admit that for all of us, this was going to be our first experience to summit the Zomba Plateau. At our age, we had known that the top of the mountain was a place for Whites and other well-to-do black families. As kids we had just enjoyed seeing the tall tower of lights turning on and off on the mountain. We watched this every night in our villages. Our elders once told us that it was a radio network, but this information may be true or may be false. People in the villages had a tendency of spreading rumors, some false, and with the passage of time they were established as true stories.

Before we departed, we were advised to bring along our tops and sweaters. We were told that it was very cold on the mountain. No wonder, on the day of the trip, some kids brought sweaters that were beyond their sizes. It was as if we were travelling to a polar region.

We rode in minibuses and we sang as we went up. We drove past Chancellor College. I tell you, even a stranger could tell that the kids, though their villages were an inch away from Chancellor College, never had a chance to explore the town. The kids were excited by the tall buildings. They pointed fingers at the buildings. The atmosphere in the cars was charged with excitement. At times they shouted to the driver to drive slowly so they could look at the buildings or something more thoroughly. Some kids had weak stomachs; time and again we had to stop for them to vomit on the roadside bush.

The cars drove up a snake-like, winding road. It was tarred. We saw the famous Mulunguzi Dam. The waters were usually calm and had an endless length. Every time we came to a thing that provoked our curiosity, the driver provided detailed information about it. I liked the way he did it. The cars drove, drove, drove and drove. Finally we arrived at our destination. It was flat and green throughout.

There were a lot of activities. John did not forget to bring our usual Frisbee. To this day I recall what was written on this yellow Frisbee: NO SLIP GRIP. We threw and threw and threw. Before we drove back, we received some sports shirts. They were labeled "AMERICAN YOUTH SOCCER ORGANIZATION (AYSO)."

The Californian team left. At the Passion Center things seemed to move at a normal pace now. In fact, when the team was at the Passion Center, things seem to move faster than before.

The majority of the male kids had already started missing the youthful Californian boys. They were what one might say 'Our brothers from other wombs.' People talked about John, Matthew, Don and Weston. For John, there was a rumor that gained ground about him. I heard it from the mouths of two or three kids. Just like us, he too had no parents. They had passed away just like ours. But I was quicker and clever on this rumour. I told myself that this rumor may be or may not be true, that the truth actually lay in his heart.

Our brothers and sisters left a proud family in Africa. I remember one day after Pilira had returned from America, for he had visited shortly after the Californian team had left, he brought some gums and sweets. They were wrapped in papers, on which was written: 'To A Friend'.

'These sweets have been provided by your American friends. They are just kids like you. They pray for you and love you,' spoke he to us. 'What does the print on the sweets and gums mean in Chichewa?' asked he.

'*Kwa mzanga,*' translated I. My answer brought in some life after a deathly silence that had filled the Multipurpose Room when Pilira asked about the meaning of the print.

The Americans were indeed family and friends. Even the blind could see it. Some of us by then were dressed in clothes with some American labels: THE HAPPY SIDE IS THE RIVERSIDE, JUST DO IT, UCLA. It was all good. I loved my 'Just Do It' t-shirt. It was white in colour. It was not something just to put on, but to draw some inspiration from what was written on it. I felt like, as a kid in my situation, I could write a thousand-paged autobiography drawing inspiration from what was written on my t-shirt.

CHAPTER EIGHTEEN

Oh my sweet sister

It was hard to watch my sister leave when she did. Who was going to protect her from the vices of the city, the vices of Blantyre city? A million times the radio had announced the vices taking place in the big cities of our Great Nation. Was it not the same city that snatched my father from my mother? There was a highway in the city with many cars. Who was going to hold her hand when crossing the highway? All my young life she had been part of me. My sweet sister Gertrude was leaving. As she walked away step by step, it was as if I was never going to see her again. Babura's mother, from Mr. Meyer's Residence, secured her a job as a house servant in the city. She was going to work for a Dutch woman married to a Malawian husband.

On the morning she left, I cried and cried and cried as she walked before disappearing at a distant sharp bend. This bend was marked by banana stems that extended outwards towards the main dusty road.

'Bo, *mwana wabwino usalire,*' she fondly asked me to stop crying. All my young life she had been sweet to me. I remember in those days she used to teach me how to fight. She taught me how to deliver blows and kicks in fights. I remember one day my mother warned her to mind her habit of teaching me how to fight.

'If you break his ribs, you and I are going to know each other today,' my mother warned her sarcastically from the cooking hut.

'Ma, we are just playing. She is not going to hurt me,' I said innocently.

'Shut up! Upright ears! You and your fellow millipede better stop what you are doing,' she roared and she threw a cob at us. Its few grains jumped with force when it hit the wall. It bounced back and missed my sister's nose by a very thin boundary.

So my sister was slowly going to disappear at the sharp bend. I likened her disappearance to the disappearance of a little, orphan girl in one of the clan tales my other sister told me the other night. This innocent little orphan was swallowed by an evil river. She got slowly engulfed by the rising river. A sad-toned song struck me:

> *Aaa ah Chenjera kambalame*
> Be alert little bird
> *Chenjera!*
> Be alert!
> *Amayi anandiwuza!*
> Mother said!

Chenjera Kambalame!!

Be alert little bird

Chenjera!

Be alert

Ndikazafa Ine

When I die

Chenjera Kambalame

Be alert little bird

Chenjera

Be alert

Udzapite kwa mlongo wako!

Go to your brother!

Chenjera Kambalame

Be alert little bird

Chenjera!

Be alert!

My eyes got heavy and my eyelids got soaked. My sight could not take me beyond the bananas to see her again.

The sharp corners of her departure pierced my young life like the pains of the night. Yes, the pains of the night. They were the pains that would have given me a permanent ridge of scars across my back. My trail of life is not of memories but miseries.

Let me share with you, though it is hard to write line after line, and as I am putting these lines down my eyes are heavy with tears. The blanket that I got from GAIA had worn out. The threads hung loose and dangled when I tried to lift it in motion. The way the threads were scattered, you could see a rat in the roof while covering your face with the blanket. In the cold months, where the dew dripped off the edge of the roof to the floor, I was cold on the sackcloth I was sleeping on.

So an idea struck me. I gathered metallic pins to stitch it together. I pinned all the loose threads together, especially the middle section. This marked another problem. Every time I went to bed, the pins scratched my back. When I woke up, the pinned area got stiff due to the dried blood I shed as the pins scratched me. I wished humans could have the privilege of a third eye at the back so that I could see my own dying back. Each time I saw my blanket stiffening with my own blood, I felt my life falling apart. It was as if a finish line for my life had been drawn. My very soul was troubled and I saw death crawling into my life.

Right away I said a prayer of thanks when we received new blankets at the Passion Center. In fact, a cold season had come and that was a reason why we received new blankets. I carefully folded the old blanket neatly and turned it into my pillow. I was careful to bury the pins underneath as I was folding it.

So the size of this night pain was equal to the sharp pain in my heart caused by the departure of my sister. She disappeared around the sharp bend.

CHAPTER NINETEEN

My people and their ways

Somewhere in a year, it would get dry. Trees shed their leaves. In such a season, the sun ruthlessly roasted the Earth. It was said to be the period after harvesting. When people had harvested, it was dusty in the land. Whirlwinds were a common sight in recently cleared gardens.

After each harvesting, people cleared graveyards. Each compound owned its own graveyard. The *Mwinimbumba* of our compound never waited for the ancestors to trouble him in his dreams and visions, he made sure we cleared our graveyard once in a full year. It was widely held in the land that a graveyard is a home of *amanda*, the spirits of the dead. They were the Living Dead bridging us to *Mulungu,* God. As kids we were also able to know that *amanda* could bring a curse or luck to our compound. It all depended on our standing with them.

Such beliefs were unquestionable. When a grey-haired elder said that the Spirits dwell in that big tree or in that dark cave or in that big rock or in that big river, it was unquestionable truth. It became a part of us.

So one morning, a compound gathered and cleared its graveyard. Tombs were earthed up and there were huge mounds of earth in the graveyard. Before the sun got to the over-head a company would gather in their compound. In it people took some *thobwa*, sweet beer.

I clearly recall, in our compound elders sat in a place of honor. They made their own line as they sat on pieces of wood or worn out wooden vessels. A big cup of *thobwa* would start on one end of the line. They passed it on to each other until everyone had dipped his mouth in it.

Children, too, had their own line. If you sipped you passed the cup on to the person next to you. That was how we feasted. It was widely believed that the harmony and peace of a compound lay in feasting from the same cup and plate.

Women endlessly filled the cups until the compound enjoyed the very heart of the feast.

It was also in the same dry season where masked dancers, *Nyau*, ran about and danced. Initiation ceremonies were also a common sight in the land after harvesting. Both grown-up boys and girls attended the initiation ceremonies.

The masked dancers ran and danced in the villages. Whistles were on their mouths and anklets made sound as they ran. They were dressed in skirts of grass and dried banana leaves. Their heads were covered with hats made of painted chicken feathers. They danced for the

Jando, a male initiation ceremony. The dancers carried sticks and hit chickens that ran in their paths. They danced on a cleared small patch of land.

Ngaliba, an instructor for a male initiation, usually looked fierce in his dance wear. His body was covered in wet red earth dug from the village creek. He had fresh blood on his lips. In one hand he carried a large hat made of chicken feathers and a small wooden axe in the other. On his head he carried an embalmed *ntchezi*, a water rat. The *ntchezi* was balanced on his head with a string that extended from the hat of feathers he wore. He appeared from the distant bananas trees with another high rank of masked dancers. Rattles of wild seeds that were bound to their legs made noise as they ran.

All the masked dancers and the initiates lined up and danced. The stomachs and faces of the initiates were painted white, red and yellow. They danced forward and backward, as if in a tribal conquest dance, and the narrow long drums were being beaten. They collectively raised their sticks, machetes and small wooden axes. There were engulfed in the crowd of dust that rose from the ground as they hit hard the ground with their feet. They later retired to the *simba*, initiation shelter. The *simba* was built in a hidden site near a river

I remember, the initiated boastingly proclaimed many things about the *simba*. It made you feel empty. It made you feel immature and that you had not experienced many things in this world. The initiated gossiped many things. There was honey on a tea spoon. No man managed to eat all of it. The more one tried to swallow of it, the more it kept refilling itself on the spoon.

'What about that story of a three-legged goat, the great wrestler of all generations?' the initiated had said. It wrestled against men for many ages, but it had never been brought down to the ground.

Such stories created inquisitiveness in the minds of the immature. They also wanted to go into the *simba* to see for themselves. They wanted to wrestle against the great wrestler and taste the honey. By these two, they were going to achieve seniority and maturity in the society.

My grandmother was *Namkungwi*, an instructor for female initiation, *chabulika*. She had deputies: a drum beater and an orator. These were old women from nearby compounds. At times I had seen her team being hired in distant lands to initiate girls when the harvest moon appeared.

In the days prior to the initiation ceremony, grown-up girls, initiated first, danced *chitekwere* in our compound. *Chitekwere* was a dance performed by initiated girls in preparation for an initiation ceremony.

`Bidi! Bidi! Bidi!'

That was the echo of a long drum awaking the land. The grown-up girls danced on an open ground in the silvery moonlight. They danced on a cleared small piece of land in front of my grandmother's house.

`Bidi! Bidi! Bidi!' the echo went all the time. The echo actually made our compound famous. Initiated girls were swallowed in it as they danced excitedly.

Awigiwee!!
Pereka mtondo wotukwanira!!
Awigiwe!!
Pereka mtondo wotukwanira!

The women wagged their bottoms. They moved their waists to and fro. Their waists were tied with pieces of cloth.

The actual day for initiation was a great day for the women. It was the launching day. Our compound got as busy as an ant-hill. It was engulfing female visitors from distant lands. At night, the initiates sang as they got to the mouth of our compound.

Nguluwe ndi anache!
Eeeh Eeeh!!
Nguluwe ndi anache
Woooowoooo!!!!

Lero sitigona
Wooo wooo!!!
Tigona chiimire!
Wooo! Wooo!!

Men were not allowed in the hidden female initiation site. It was widely held that, if a man set his feet in the hidden initiation site, he was going to develop swollen legs and he was going to be barren. In fact, all the compound boys had relocated to a hut on the far end of the compound.

There was a story of a certain drunkard who deliberately went in the female initiation ceremony. I cannot mention his name for privacy's sake. He was a funny man. He tied his bottom with a wrapper just as women do. He stood with the women in a circle as the initiates danced in the center.

However his nostrils and mouth sent some sharp smell of native beer and his mouth had some less of the native beer. They were soon onto him. They grabbed him and threw him on the ground. They grabbed him again and dragged him on the ground. He left a trail with his feet as they dragged him. They cursed him and his mother as well.

'Go and watch your mother's private parts!' they shouted angrily. 'Go and watch what she does with your father in bed.'

There is no fiction about this story, not at all. This is what I saw with my own naked eyes on that silvery moonlight. I saw it when they dragged him to the mouth of the compound where we had relocated.

CHAPTER TWENTY

The famous class

The dry and rainy seasons came and disappeared. Each of the seasons would disappear quietly, so quietly as if they never existed. Calm was restored in the land after the recent excitement of the initiation ceremonies and other traditional feasts. Mulunguzi Primary School and the Passion Center were permanently there, be it rainy or dry season. Each time I looked at them they stood calmly as if they had grown tap roots that powerfully stood in the ground.

Sometime in a year was the rainy season. There were rains in the late days of 2006, jumping into the new year of 2007. I was now in Standard Eight. It was a famous class just like Standard Three and Standard Five. One might ask why these classes were so famous.

I am sure I have already talked about Standard Three earlier, so let me share about Standard Five and Standard Eight. If I remember correctly Standard Five was where students learnt about the definition of `agriculture' for the first time. The term `agriculture' made Standard Five a noteworthy year in general. Was it because agriculture is the backbone of the economy of our great nation?

Once you were about to start Standard Five, other learners would ask you 'Do you know the definition of agriculture?' It's no wonder a learner could recite the definition without knowing the spelling of each word that made up the definition. Even I had mastered reciting the definition from memory before I attended the very first lesson of Standard Five: 'Agriculture is the practice of growing crops and rearing animals on land for people's use.' This was the excitement that filled every learner of Standard Five.

Standard Eight was a very senior class. In fact, it was the last class of Primary education. Learners were supposed to write National Examinations. This was not an ordinary test where a teacher would write questions on a board. No, the exams were in printed state, and they were printed elsewhere beyond the edges of the African land mass. They were printed in a White man's land, Britain. Just by being printed in Britain, this added a considerable weight to the National Examinations.

Of course the element of mental colonialism could not be singled out, but you know how sometimes the element of mental colonialism makes our people have a high opinion towards things of western origin. These exams were widely called 'exams whose papers smelled like a white man's perfume.' It was said that perfume was smeared on to them as they printed the exams.

It was a year of studying and studying and studying. I wanted to get accepted into a secondary school. I wanted to follow the path of my brother, Godfrey. He was already in a secondary school and the Passion Center paid his school fees. At the Passion Center they said I could be a pilot if I got selected for a good secondary school.

This was what I did: each morning I would wake up early and prepare myself. I boiled my water on burning maize stalks or small, dry sticks. I made sure to go earlier to attend part-time classes administered by Mr. Kapesi. He was a famous teacher in our day at our school. He lived in the trading town and each morning he cycled his bicycle past our compound. I knew him as a man of his word. If he said 'no entrance to anyone else once I enter the classroom,' it was as clear as in writing. In his words there was a solid fact, just as the undisputed fact that the sun rises from the east.

So I would run and run and run to get in the doorway before he landed on it himself. I mostly ran through shortcuts. However, the paths were not safe during the rainy seasons. They were banked by tall green maize. The banks of maize left a very narrow space giving way for the paths. There were also some short plants that closed in the path as they grew from both banks. Each morning you walked in the narrow paths, your feet got wet due to the morning dew. The wet leaves slapped your feet every time you walked. By the time you got to school your feet were trembling because they had gotten cold.

During the day, I went to a nearby small hill that was enclosed by banana trees which stood in a creek. It was always as quiet as the grave so I peacefully buried myself into books. In the young darkness of evenings, I read and read and read tirelessly. I used a *koloboyi* that gave dim light from its burning string soaked in a small tank of paraffin. I was limited in how often I could use it because it was a family *koloboyi*. One or two times it was taken away to be used in the cooking hut.

A wonderful plan struck me one day. I went to my uncle, Mr. James Mbewe. He was a gentle man, but principled, and he lived by his word just like my primary school teacher, Mr. Kapesi. He was medium height with slight baldness. On your first day meeting him, he could dominate the whole conversation. He was the kind of man who liked to skirt round when he was about to mention something of importance. As he skirted around he was mindful of the main idea. He was artistic in his style. He slightly wondered away, as if to gather energy with which to strike the main point.

In those days he worked in the English Department at Chancellor College. So on that evening I told my story wholeheartedly. I needed my own *koloboyi* to study at night. He was deeply impressed. It was clearly written all over his face, I could tell. I even felt it in his remarks. A million times he said 'That is a wise idea.'

He gave me some money. It covered the amount of a *koloboyi*, but also there was extra with which to fill the tank with paraffin.

On the next day I went to the nearby small trading town, Chinamwali. I went with the clever Phuzo. He also wanted to buy one. We bought those *koloboyis* that had an electric bulb. The bulb-vacuum acted as a filling tank. Its mouth had a metal pad skillfully fitted to it. The mouth of the pad-ring met a metallic cap that had a nozzle on its surface. The nozzle extended from the middle of the cap pointing to the sky. A thick-plaited string extended through the nozzle to the bottom of the bulb.

Every time you wanted to refill your paraffin, you just pulled the cap. The paraffin seller inserted a funnel through the bulb mouth and supplied the paraffin, which soaked the string. When you wanted to use the *koloboyi*, you just brought a burning match stick or a dried stalk to the knot of the string at the nozzle. The soaked string gave light throughout until the paraffin ran dry and you had to refill your tank.

At times I had enough money to have some paraffin in store. I had it on standby in a glass bottle. I always sealed the mouth of the glass with a maize cob to keep my paraffin safe.

CHAPTER TWENTY-ONE

Papers that smelled like a white man's perfume

On weekends many things happened at home. We would either receive visitors or go to the river and dig sand for school.

At some point my grandmother, from my father's side, visited our compound. She was very beautiful and light-skinned. Her cheeks were decorated with traditional tattoos. The pattern of the traditional tattoos and the few openings between her lower front teeth increased her beauty every time she smiled.

She shed tears at the sight of me. In fact, it had been many ages since she last saw me. This she told me. For me, this was my first time meeting her. She carried me on her legs as she shed tears uncontrollably. 'When I die, I ask you to unveil my tomb,' she said, touching my hand. I did not know what to say so I just tried to avoid her soaked eyes.

One other time, I saw a white man coming to our compound. It was his first time here and it was my first time to meet him. His name was Phillip Thesing. We fondly called him Phil. From the scraps of my sister's narration, I learnt that this was the man taking care for her in the city. He was sponsoring her to attend school. Just like a white man at the Passion Center, he also brought his camera. There was a clicking sound in the compound. As kids we stood our best styles for the photos.

Even members of neighboring compounds rushed to our compound to see the white man. The rumor about him spread to neighboring compounds in the way bush fire spreads on dry grass in the midst of dry season. So neighbors were drawn to our compound in the way water rushes into an empty cup dipped in a huge pot filled with water to the brim.

I soon got used to him. He called me by name every time he wanted to address me. It was all nice. I thought of his name, Thesing. It ended in 'ing' and in school we were taught that any word ending in 'ing' was a verb. Was this man's name a verb? Or do Americans not care much about names? He was an American. I had a million questions emanating from the nature of his name.

I was glad when this inquisitiveness out of nowhere died out, and I focused on what was going on in the compound. If you did something he desired, he raised his hand and said 'High five!' as you shook hands. In fact, there was one clear impression I made of him. He believed in doing x when it was time for x. With him, no one must jump to y when it was still time for x.

Before he left, he gave me a torch. It had a strong ray of light. At night it sent a ray of light in the sky as far as your eyes could travel. In the dark, I liked how the ray turned my thumb pink when I brought my finger to the glass. When I ran short of paraffin, the torch kept me going.

On those same weekends we went to the river. We went to dig sand for the school building project. It was an individual effort that involved each learner to benefit the school. The classrooms that were at window level were yet to be completed.

So it was posted in plain language: NO SAND NO CLASSES. We went to the shallow sandy sections to dig sand into our tins. Each Monday before entering class, you were supposed to throw your portion on a huge heap. The heap was piling up so quickly as if it were going to touch the sky. Its bottom had been enclosed with bricks. Once you threw your sand, a teacher ticked your name to attend classes for that week.

As a school, it was as if we all had the same spirit. A spirit which made us say 'This is our school. We have it, but also we should build it.'

No wonder, later, when the sonorous gong was stolen, the idea to employ a watchman was wholeheartedly agreed upon. Each month, every learner was supposed to pay a watchman fee. The fee was at K10, roughly the same cost as a pencil in our day. Those were the days when money had weight.

Exam time came. We went to a neighboring school to be arranged in seats for the national examinations. Our school was not an examination center. So we had to walk to the neighboring Matiti Primary School. From my earlier impression, Matiti was a bigger school than ours. For instance, when it was time to receive pencils, pens and notebooks at our school, senior boys were sent to get the items from Matiti Primary School. They also had more buildings than us. But we beat them in one thing: they had only one *mjigo* for water.

After arranging the desks and seating plan, we went back to the Passion Center. In fact there were about five or six of us from the Passion Center who were sitting for the exams that year. At the Passion Center, they prayed for us. We were also encouraged to get focused. It topped off my courage and hope. Before we went home, they gave us some pens and rulers.

CHAPTER TWENTY-TWO

I am selected for secondary school

Yes. We grew deep into the heart of the holiday. The exam anxiety had now grown faint, so faint as if it had gone for a lifetime away. But I still knew that one day, the results would be out, and the exam anxiety again would get fresh, so fresh as if we just wrote them yesterday and today the results were out.

On most mornings, I fed the goats. Each time the morning sunrays penetrated the canopy of tree leaves enveloping our compound, I went into the bush. In the bush, I broke branches of succulent trees. I either tied them with a wild creeper or the fresh, thin bark of banana tree stems. I tied them into a bundle and carried them to our compound.

At times, I cut fresh banana leaves for feeding. I cut them from neighboring gardens that were bordered by banana trees.

Before the sun rose overhead, I walked to the Passion Center. At times, I walked with Ashley. She was a young American missionary volunteering at the Passion Center and a nearby Christian school, Chirunga Transhaven Private Secondary School.

This time around, the Bible classes were conducted in two groups; the Kids group and the Youth group. Either Uncle Joe or Uncle Stewart worked with the kids. Uncle Titi, Ashley, and Auntie Irene worked with the youth. Actually, over the years, the Passion Center saw new staff members coming in. Each staff influenced the kids with the career at which she or he was a specialist. Auntie Irene talked about kids becoming agricultural specialists. Uncle Titi talked of kids becoming electricians.

I was in the Youth group. Our group gathered under a mango tree. It stood behind the Multipurpose Room. Its broad leaves cast a dense shadow. In our group they talked about many things: careers, growing up, and changing.

The children gathered in the Multipurpose Room. At times they played outdoor games. There was one game that when I watched them playing, brought me back to old days. It brought me back to the days when I had just gotten into the Passion Center.

Uncle Joe stood at the front. They stretched out their hands and stood still. The rule of the game was to pay attention to what Uncle Joe instructed in the front. When he said `do *this*', you were supposed to move your hands in an imitation of him. If he said `do *that*,' you were not supposed to imitate his hand motion. If you did imitate at the mention of `do *that*,' you were booted out of the game. The game went on like that until the champion was found. It was so interesting.

Days hatched into weeks, and weeks into months since we wrote the exams. One day a rumor flew in the land. It was a rumor that the exams results were now ripe. It was in the next day when we learnt that the rumor had some truth to it. The results were posted on the school board. People were drawn to the school to see the results. I was one of the eight students who were selected by good secondary schools in the district, and would be in the Southern part of Malawi. I was selected to attend Masongola Secondary school. It was my brother's school. He was now going into Form Three.

I was excited, and excitement engulfed the Passion Center. I joined a few other Passion Center students already in secondary schools. I thought of my friend John. I wished I could ship a letter to him to let him know that I was now going to a secondary school. Oh, my brother across the Atlantic waters.

The story about my selection to a government secondary school was everywhere in our village and even in some villages next to it. Rumor is a great traveler. The story about my selection travelled as fast as the sharp echo of a sonorous gong in calm air.

On one evening I went to Mr. Mbewe's compound. He shook my hand in a congratulatory way. He told others in the neighboring doors that I had been selected to a secondary school. `A compound with educated people commands respect in a society,' spoke he. `When a white man comes to your compound, people do have confidence that there is someone who is going to speak with him. There is shame in sending for an educated person from another compound to speak for the uneducated when a white man comes to their compound,' added he while his face beamed with excitement. I saw it on his face from the burning *koloboyi*.

He was a man who was always delighted to see children progressing academically. He was the same man who planted a craving for reading in my life. He sowed a reading seed in my heart. Not that he just sowed it. No, he did what any good farmer would do. He time and again watered that seed by supplying me with children's books. He encouraged me to read children's books that he brought me from his office. They were interesting books and I liked them. Most of them they were about animal tales, and my favorite clever Hare existed in many of them.

Sometimes he narrated me stories he read in other books. I liked his art of storytelling so much. The energy he wore and atmosphere he brought as he was telling stories could clearly make your mind's eyes visualize events as they unfolded. He could skillfully skirt and skirt and skirt round, capturing your whole mind, before striking the main detail in the story. He once told me about the folk tale of `A Blind Man and A Lame Man.' It was about how the lame man exploited the blind man. It was an interesting story and I kept on asking him about the plot of the story time and again. To quench my inquisitiveness about the story line, he promised to bring it to me someday. He wanted me to read it on my own to appreciate it.

Yes, our compound was swallowed to the core with happiness. Even a distant relative was stirred in excitement for my selection. But I looked at my worn out blanket. Should I take it to a boarding school? No, I answered myself. Did I have a suitcase in which to bring my few clothes? No, I also asserted to myself.

Then a wonderful plan struck me. I had built confidence in that old saying: he who hesitates is lost. One afternoon I was at a red gate. I banged on the gate of Mrs. E Ntaukira. *Di! di! di! di!* The outside of my hand landed on the reddish gate. I paused for a response. *Di! di! di!* I hit it again.

`Yes!' a soft voice sneaked through the sitting room windows. It was her. I calmed myself and cleared my throat. `It is you,' she said while smiling. 'Congratulations,' she continued while shaking my hand and patting my back.

We sat on the verandah. She created a rapport for me to narrate my story.

'My blanket is old and frayed. I can even see a rat in the roof when I cover my face,' I tried to be a joker, but that was the method to my madness. 'Even if I decided to carry it to a boarding school, I would have to carry it in my hands as I do not have a suitcase,' I disclosed sadly, but I tried to speak with energy.

In the end, she said 'Okay I have heard you.' It injected confidence in me. A few days later she called me to get two thick blankets and a red and black suitcase.

CHAPTER TWENTY-THREE

A new chicken in a pen

It was a day or two before our departure to the secondary school. And it was at the beginning of the year, so it was a rainy season.

Through my brother, Godfrey, I learnt that roasted maize and groundnuts were a favorite food for students in boarding schools. So we pushed the grass-thatch of a granary with a stick. Then we took out maize and shelled it. We also opened sacks to take out some groundnuts kept from the previous harvesting season. The maize and groundnuts were roasted and roasted and roasted until I filled my own flat, round basket. Our baskets, made of bamboo, creepers and palm leaves, were filled to the brim.

We did not forget to roast a chicken on glowing embers. A strand of wire was placed over cooking stones and charcoal smoldered in its midst. The chicken was placed on the strand of wire. Salt and pepper were added and it turned brown.

On the day of departure, my heart was filled with both excitement and sadness. I was sad to leave my home and friends, but at the same time I was excited to go to a secondary school. A few members of my compound and friends escorted us part of the way. My grandmother was there, too. She walked with a broken heart. Both of her hands were behind her back. One was folded and touched the elbow of the other that dangled just below her buttocks. Her head was covered in a cloth. Another piece of cloth ran over her shoulder and hung loosely at the bottom.

She was worried. She had heard of teasing and bullying at secondary schools. New students in secondary schools were being harassed by older students. I tried hard not to show that I realized that she was worried about me. I tactfully looked at her through the corners of my eyes. As I walked, a sad song of a clan tale struck me. I felt so low. A few months ago it rang in my head as my sister was leaving.

Aaa ah Chenjera kambalame
Be alert bird
Chenjera!
Be alert!
Amayi anandiwuza!
Mother said!
Chenjera Kambalame!!
Be alert bird
Chenjera!
Be alert

Ndikazafa Ine
When I die
Chenjera Kambalame
Be alert bird
Chenjera
Be alert
Udzapite kwa mlongo wako!
Go to your brother!
Chenjera Kambalame
Be alert bird
Chenjera!
Be alert!

We followed the dusty road, heading up. As we trod, it grew more and more hilly. It was as if the village were sinking below. At a certain slope, it displayed beautiful scenery as we got higher and higher. The beautiful view was topped by scattered patches of red earth that were in some gardens.

Everyone turned back. There were now three of us: Godfrey, Milles, and I. Milles lived in the next compound, and just like me, she had been selected to Masongola secondary school. My mind wholeheartedly rested on my new school. My worry for my grandmother had now grown faint, and the worry to leave my friends, too, had grown distant. The sad tone clan song was now a distant echo. I was glad.

We got to the school. Masongola Secondary School was my new school now. Its motto was `On We Go.' Others would add `Forward Ever, Backward Never.'

The Passion Center had already paid our school fees, so Godfrey and I got our mattresses when we arrived. Soon we were in the section of hostels. There were three male hostels named after famous African rivers: Niger, Zambezi and Nile. Female students had one hostel, Shire. I clearly recall, the rain was falling in showers. We were put into Zambezi Hostel. It was the biggest hostel of all. That was where my brother was located. He kept an eye on me until I met my guardian. Each new student was assigned to a senior student to take care of them. Male students we called fathers while female students they called mothers.

In Zambezi hostel, it was a tense atmosphere. The walls were stained with many writings. Walls were labeled with either markers or chalk or charcoal. *Poison oz here b4 u*, on one part it read. On a worn out ceiling it read *Welcom 2 Hell: The Guantanamo Bay Detention.*

I could hear senior boys singing in the distance. Their voices drew nearer and nearer to the hostel area. `Form Ones! We are going to kill you tonight! We will eat you alive. Monkeys! Your tails are blocking our corridors!' It sent fear through me. When I was a little kid, I heard that white people eat black people, but if I might claim to have ever seen one munched alive, honestly I would be telling a lie. Here I heard my breath ready to witness a black man munch a fellow black man. But I did not know whether I was really going to witness this daylight witchcraft, let alone if I were one of those to be munched.

Godfrey had just stepped away to welcome a friend. It was not easy for you to walk about. A short distance could last you hours and hours as you were stopped a million times to answer questions. Most of these questions were silly to make you look stupid.

'Hey, Form One!' They would not address you by your name but by the class you were in. 'What is your name?'

'And where do you come from?'

'And how are you going to entertain us?' Many questions showered down on me. There were about four or five of them. 'Why are you in Form One? Of all these classes, why did you choose to be in Form One?'

'Prophet Dauda', I tried to respond following the order of the questions.

'Prophet? Isaiah? Moses? You think this is a church? Are you here to do the work of God?' This one had a broken voice and he spoke hoarsely. He could scare you on your first day.

'Prophecy for us, man of God!' someone shouted from a top bed. This made me, for the first time, hate the one who gave me the name of Prophet at home.

'What is that boy saying?' That was another senior boy. I was totally confused.

'He says his name is Prophet.'

'What? Come here right away!' I trembled with fear, partly from a chill from the showers. I tried to move a few steps to follow where he called me.

'Hey boy, are we done?' asked the student who held me in the beginning. 'Little rat!'

'Hey, I said come here!' roared the one who called me. I was caught in between. Should I go and disobey this one? Or I should I not go and disobey that one? I was weighing the options within myself. I staged a show for them and they liked it. This one finally let me go to the other student.

'Go and wash this plate for me first.' He handed me the plate. I washed it quickly and faithfully. 'Yes. So what is your name?' he asked as if he did not hear it in the first place.

'Prophet Dauda" I replied.

'Is Prophet your name?

'Yes.' There was noise everywhere in the hostel and outside. Continuing students welcomed each other noisily. At the same time there was noise from the show that was staged by the questioning of the new students. In one place continuing students commanded a newcomer to take off his one shoe. They made him speak through it, the same way one does with a cell phone, to tell his parents that he had arrived well and that he was enjoying his first day of school.

'Have you ever been in a class of English before?' he continued.

'Yes' I answered with no interest. How could one get selected to a secondary school without passing through a class of English in Malawi, a country once owned by the Queen of Britain?

'What type of a noun is Prophet?' he carried on with the inquiry.

'Common noun,' I answered. Others laughed uncontrollably. Maybe I was becoming stupid, I thought.

'Have you ever had sex?' his friend asked from his bed. I was silent. 'Form One I am asking you!' I was scared. The noise grew louder and louder.

'Who is your father?'

'Joseph Nyirenda,' I replied.

'Hoho! The Lion. He treated me like trash when I was just a newcomer,' spoke one tall boy out of nowhere. He was just passing by in the corridor. He entered the room where I was being questioned. 'Which hostel are you allocated in?'

'I don't know yet"

'What? You don't know? You are going to daydream. Lie on the bed and dream your hostel name and say it.' He was serious.

If it were not for the boarding master, they would have carried on with the show. They heard that he was coming to the hostel section and they escaped.

I met my father on the night of the same day. We slept in Zambezi Room 10.

When it was approaching dawn, I heard a shout. 'Form One!! Get to the corridor!' The voice pierced the cold air. It was unclear outside due to the earlier rains. 'I have no time. This is only your first night. If I come over and see that you are still sleeping I will slap you!' the caller continued. 'Or have you already familiarized yourself with the campus, and you know all the angles to play tricks on me? I said wake up and get to the corridor!'

My father shook me. 'Wake up. Go to the corridor. They should *teach* you how to do some work.' We lined up in the corridor.

'Some of you will not make it to universities,' the caller began. He was gentle in his speaking and excited. 'So we teach you to do some work here in case you don't go far with school.' There was a sense of drama in his mouth, demonstrating the art of skirting round the main point before finally striking it.

So we cleaned the toilets, rooms and the outside. Joseph and I relocated to Nile Room 6 when it was completely clean. It was the room that the boarding master allocated us to.

CHAPTER TWENTY-FOUR

A calf grows with strikes from the herder's stick

With the morning sun, we ate our breakfast. The bell rang. *Ngili! ngili! ngili!!* It sent students into the hall. It was a different bell from that gong under the tree at Mulunguzi Primary School. This bell was a medium-sized golden cup with a loose rod inside. It had a short wooden handle. With passage of time I learnt that all the activities were run on the high-pitched tone of the innovative bell. Its sharp echo marked the shift from this activity to the next on the school ground. And only the head boy (male president) and the head girl (female president) rang the bell. The school management was strict on that. So every time it rang, the whole school was sure to shift to the next item on the schedule. At my former school, the schedule could get compromised because the gong was prone to many unauthorized student ringings. Naughty students aimed at the gong from a distance with stones.

Of course there was a heavy gong at the campus. It was an old wheel tied to a tree branch that was near the cafeteria. Every time your ears caught the sound of the gong, you just knew it was time to fill your belly.

In the school hall, the assembly setting was different from that of Mulunguzi Primary School. During the assembly all the students were seated on chairs. At my former school, we were outside and standing on our feet.

On this day, all the Form One students were sitting in front. The way the continuing students looked at us sent shivers through us.

After a long welcome speech, we were dismissed into our classrooms. I belonged to Form 1B. In this class, students learnt technical subjects: Technical Drawing, Metal Work and Wood Work. In our class, the desks were slanted and they stood above our hips. The chairs took the height of the slanted edge.

Certain cursive writings greeted us on the board in front. At the end of each word, there was a percentage assigned to it. I can confidently recall the first two or three writings.

Work	99%
Food	0.5%
Education	0.5%

After a week or two, I was able to understand what all those writings stood for. It really depicted the life of a Form One student. And most times, we gathered in small bands to share the humiliation we were going through. It was all because we were in Form One. The whole thing was what we called 'when a new chicken joins other chickens in a pen, it is welcomed by a fight.'

A Form One student would open his day as a worker. 'Form One! Get to the corridor!' That was his alarm every dawn. 'I should not count up to three before you line up in the corridor!' The alarm would keep wailing. That would probably be from any senior student or a hostel prefect, but with passage of time, there was a Form One student who was picked to do that job.

We would run to the corridor. We operated within our groups, and as groups we rotated in cleaning the hostel. One day, the toilets were for this group, and tomorrow the toilets were for that group. It also applied in the rooms and outside the hostel.

After the cleaning, we took a cold shower, before the senior students woke up. That was the shower time for Form One. If you failed to bathe during this time, you would wait for the next dawn. It was widely held that 'a son cannot shower at the same time as his father.' They said to see your father's manhood organ would be disrespectful at its peak. Only Lot's Ham would do that, and he was cursed.

The washing was done, and then we took our plates to the cafeteria. It was put in stupid language by the senior students: 'Form Ones go and bother the cook. At your sight they will wake up and see that it is time to serve breakfast.'

It was a custom. As a Form One boy, you were supposed to carry plates for the senior students. Every time you passed by a room, your pile grew faster. The pile was stacking up as if it was going to rise beyond your head. At the cafeteria, you were supposed to stand in the doorway and hand the plates to the senior students as they passed. If it was lunch or supper time, they would line you up and make sure you tucked in your shirts. You remained in the line until all the senior students were served. You were mostly served last.

Eating breakfast was done. We went to the hostel to drop off the plates, but the paths for Nile and Niger were the toughest during meal times. The paths were stony and senior students loved to sit on them as they ate. So they threw their plates on the paths and you had to re-collect the pile for washing. That was during the day.

After evening studies, you would also hear the shout again. 'Form One! Get to the corridor! I should not count one to three before you line up!'

Cleaning after evening studies was tough. The majority of continuing students were in the hostels, and they would expose you to harassment of all kind.

'When you have lined up, don't lean against our wall,' a continuing student would walk behind you. 'You could bring down the wall,' he said.

'And don't forget each year we conduct a sacrificial ceremony. We kill a Form One student and bury him in those bananas,' he would say, pointing at the bananas that stood a few meters away. 'But we have not yet identified the one to die. So individually you must ask yourself whether you are the one to be sacrificed.' By then we were standing still, as if we were lifeless objects erected on the ground. At times, a student would weigh our manhood organs with his open hand. He said he wanted to know who was a 'strong man' and a 'weak man.'

That was the life of a Form One student on Sundays, Mondays, Tuesdays, Wednesdays, Thursdays and Saturdays. I have skipped Fridays. Yes, most Fridays were days of their own. On most Fridays we created what we fondly called an 'Ocean.'

To create an 'ocean,' a hose pipe was fitted to a running tap. The waters were channeled to all the rooms. They could go as high as above your ankles. The waters were all over in the rooms, and we brushed the floor. The brushes had hairs that were hard and stiff.

It was hard to clean while the seniors were watching you from above from their beds. 'Form

One! Clean and clean and clean until the floor gets clean as a baby's private's parts! Have you ever seen a baby's private parts?'

When a senior student wanted to go to the toilet, he jumped on your back. He did not want to step in the muddy water on the floor. That was a life of a Form One in our day, but I am sure for a modern student it is a new dawn. It is the eve of Human Rights.

To you, my day may sound like a hard age. Yes, it was, but after two, three weeks we got used to it. It was all captured in the saying, 'a calf grows with strikes from the herder's stick.'

In fact it had grown on us and we got used to it. In our small bands we sat and shared our experience as the Form Ones. 'Last night there was *bakha bakha*,' one would throw out and we all laughed. *Bakha bakha* involved quacking as the ducks do. You sat in the middle while the senior students were watching you from above, and you started quacking at the same time. It was funny throughout. The heavier you quacked, the more satisfied the senior students became and they let you go.

I remember at one point, we would 'disappear' in our hostel. It involved crawling under the beds. The way the beds stood, they formed a space like an inlet in the doorway. On the opposite side, they acted as an outlet. So you disappeared through the inlet. Under the beds you crawled and crawled and crawled. You followed the tunnel underneath until you came to the outlet. By the time you reappeared, your body was covered in dust.

Yes, that was our day. I do not and I will never look at the senior boys as evil boys. They came, in their first year, innocent. They were as innocent as myself, but their new school molded them into who they were. Even myself as an upperclassman, I felt no guilt in making a Form One feel like he was a Form One. I went away without a sense of guilt every time I made a Form One student sweep or quack or disappear. After all of it, you resumed a normal life as if nothing had happened. You never felt remorse.

CHAPTER TWENTY-FIVE

More American missionaries

Months were so quickly swallowed, flying again to the months of June and July. People had finished harvesting, some villagers had cleared out their gardens, and it was partially clear in the land. On open ground, whirlwinds sent dust, old leaves and paper high in the sky.

Again we had a group of Americans at the Passion Center. This time around, the members were from different states. There were some from California, and others were from Ohio. Were Branton Wiseman and Emily Barker not from Georgia? What about Kathryn Dixon, was she not from Colorado? She told me that Thornton was the village she was from.

Yes it was a mixed group. Mixed as they were, they were all tied with one knot, the Great Slogan: 'Caring for the Whole Child, For The Whole Life, In the Whole Community.'

My friend John was not present among the Californians, but his sister, Kathryn, did come. My close friend Gaby Canalizo introduced her to me.

'You remember John?' asked Gaby.

'Yes for sure,' I replied.

'This is his sister,' she said while pointing at Kathryn. She was standing next to Stuphy, Trey's girlfriend.

'Hello. I am Kathryn Dixon. John talks about you guys all the time.' She extended her hand shyly.

'Hello. And I am Prophet,' said I. I stretched out my hand also. 'How is John?'

'He is fine. He did not make it out here. Probably he is planning to go back to school soon. He misses you guys a lot. I will tell him you said hello.' We talked for some time.

She was impressed with the beauty of Malawi and the hospitality of her people. 'This is so beautiful out here. All these mountains, that's awesome,' she said as she pointed at the mountains that stood lifeless and enclosed the land. To the north, stood Chinamwali; Ntonya to the south; and to the west, Zomba firmly spread itself, covering a huge length as if it were the famous Great Wall of China I had seen and read about in books. I was just flattered with the energy she wore as she expressed how she was impressed with the beauty of our land.

'Yeah' I replied without interest.

'You have an amazing country, my friend. It is amazing as the sun sets down the mountain. I captured some pictures,' she said excitedly.

I continued to feel flattered. Growing up in this land, a million times I had seen the sky turn pink and yellow as the sun sunk behind the mountain. There was nothing peculiar about that. It was just a sign that the light would soon give way for the dark. But on the other side of the mountain, it was time for the monkeys to bask themselves in the tender rays of the evening sun. 'Even the people here are so friendly and always smiling. When we wave at them, they wave back. That's so cute. You can't commonly see that where I am from. Most people they are themselves in the US, you know what I mean?' she said, not expecting an answer.

'Welcome to the Warm Heart of Africa,' I said with pride.

The excitement that felt like a lifetime ago was back again. A kid in the village heard that the *Azungu* were back again, and kids from all corners of the land flocked to the Passion Center. The kids wanted to sing the white man's songs and play his games. From sunrise to sunset the Multipurpose Room was a belly that swallowed children.

Within the first days, an Ohio friend joked with me 'You know nothing about the cold.' I soon learnt the word 'snow.'

'It snows in Ohio,' said Travis. 'Do you know snow? The waters freeze. Sometimes it falls from the sky. It stacks this high.' He said while raising his feet to give a height demo. 'Schools get cancelled when it snows much in Ohio.'

The Ohio missionaries sent kids into greater excitement all the time. They love their state, the natives of Ohio. As kids we surrounded them and they shouted collectively, 'Give me an O!'

'O!' we repeated.

'Give me an H!'

'H!'

'Give me an I!'

'I!'

'Give me another O!'

'O!'

'What does that spell?'

'*OHIOOOO!!!*'

Those were the natives of Ohio. Soon you would see them lined up, their hands coming up above their heads. They made an arm motion, collectively making the word 'Ohio' in the air. I personally thought of the word 'Ohio' and it made an impression. Of course Ohio is a four-letter word, but to an Ohioan, in it lies pride and it was a knot to tie them together as its natives. I was and still am impressed by the pride and unity toward the state of Ohio by most Ohioans.

What did my dear friend Molly Clearly tell me? The natives of Ohio have a clue to recognize each other in lands outside the state. When someone puts on a t-shirt with an Ohio label, one native of Ohio shouts `OH!' and the other one shouts `IO!' You just know they are both from Ohio.

Many kids stuck near Branton. He was a youth just like John. The kids liked to watch him do magic tricks. He had ropes and a ball. He brought the three ropes together of different lengths. He cut them with his fingers and made them of equal lengths. For the ball, he forced it in one ear and it came out the other ear. As it passed through your head, it changed color. It attracted many kids.

I was personally close to him. He told me that Alpharetta was the village he was from. In our free time, I asked him about his magic. Where did he consult the spirits to tell him about his tricks?

`Where did you learn them?' I wanted to know as I pointed at the ropes and the ball.

`I read them from books,' he replied. It generated inquisitiveness in me. In Africa a magician takes his knowledge from spirits. The spirits discern to him or her the roots, barks and leaves that can be combined to make tricks. In the West they read it in books?

But I was wise. I quickly accepted the fact that we are of two different worlds. I knew how harmful it was to employ an Africa-centric eye on

Americans or Europeans or Asians or Australians. Sometimes we do much harm to this world because we do not strip ourselves of a home-centric eye when we meet a person from the other side of the world. I also asked him many other questions.

'Do you still have slaves?' I was curious. In school we read about a stolen black man from Africa. He was stolen from his village and shipped across the Great Waters. In a very far away land, very far, he was sold as property. He worked for a white man.

'No. Not anymore. In the past we used to have them, but now we freed them.' There was a short silence.

'What about Osama Bin Laden,' I began on a different topic. 'Why does he hate the United States of America?'

'Osama! You know Osama Bin Laden?'

'Yes. The radio in my village talks about him.'

'He hates America because we are Christians.'

Yes so many questions on world politics. It's no wonder that after sometime he sent me a letter. I can recall one sentence in the letter in particular: *I can only imagine the great expectations you have of Barack Obama.* That was in 2009.

As we were engulfed to the core with excitement, we were given some paper. On this paper we wrote letters to our sponsors.

Dear Tom and Kristin Podgorski,

Hello, my name is Prophet Dauda. I am 14 years old. I have three older brothers and sisters. I live in Thom-Allan Village in Zomba district of Malawi, Southern Africa.

I go to Masongola Secondary School. My favorite subjects are English, History and Geography. My favorite color is grey. My favorite food is nsima with beans.

I would like you to pray for my academic excellence and a healthy life.

Your son,

Prophet.

The next week, there was VBS. I had not yet entered into translation. Of course I was able to understand and speak English, but it requires more than just these two skills to make a good translator. As an amateur you need first to watch good translators working. The more you watch, the more you learn to become a good translator. Godfrey was translating.

I was seated in one classroom. At one point Emily's team came into the classroom I sat in. When my eyes rested on her on her very first day from the USA, my heart said 'There a beautiful girl is!' I was a kid but I knew what a beautiful girl looked like. She was 16 years old.

She was taller than me. She had long brown hair. The thickness of her body was in its place and she looked perfect. How sweet it felt every time I sat next to her. I stole glances at her from the corners of my eyes. She was beautiful from all angles. At a glance, I saw her shallow dimples and thick eyebrows. Every time she smiled, her dimples slightly came in, topping her beauty. God Almighty!

'Prophet, my man!' was how she addressed me all the time. She had a tender voice, so tender that every time she spoke it felt like a gentle wind bringing cool air in the midst of a hot season.

Time and again I had tried to think of 'Prophet, my man.' Of course she said it to a kid, but it made me feel above everyone in this world. As I thought of it, I tried to add more words to it. She could have said 'Prophet, my only man on Earth.' I let the thought fill my whole mind.

I often thought of America. It must be some land with plenty of beautiful girls. And here it was running short of one of its beautiful girls. She was here in the Warm Heart of Africa, her beauty taking my eyes and mind prisoner.

CHAPTER TWENTY-SIX

My passion for History and English Literature

At school I loved English and History. These were my favorites. I had also been good at Geography, but History and English were at the very center of my heart.

I liked the subjects' substances and the teachers as well. Somewhere in Junior Level I was taught by Mr. J Mphedwa. He was a teacher who spiced up his lessons with jokes. His jokes would make you laugh until your stomach ached.

I remember him very well by a certain joke, one he learnt from his secondary school teacher. Behind a classroom board there is cooked rice, *nsima*, chicken, a good house, a beautiful wife. And a handsome husband, too.

He told us that in his day with his friends, they would try to break the board to get the nice things they heard in the joke. I now have realized one thing, a thing I did not realize when I was in his class listening to his stomach-ache provoking joke. He was not an empty joker. He was a joker who saw what came next in a learner's life. Of course the board required breaking, but not with a heavy hammer. No. The best hammer was to stay in school and study hard. That's all.

In Literature I enjoyed the lessons of Mr. E Kaundama. He was a young graduate. I had a favorite book in English Literature: *Looking for a Rain God and Other Short Stories from Africa*, selected and introduced by Ian Gordon. This collection exposed me to various prominent African writers. I appreciated Grace Ogot with her *The Empty Basket*; Doris Lessing with her *The Pig*; Ben Okri with his *In the Shadow of War*; Chinua Achebe with his *Uncle Ben's Choice*; Peter Songa with his *The Intruder*; James Ape with his *The Refugee*; Alex la Guma with his *Out of Darkness*; Aya Kwei Ama with his *Asemka*; Harma Tuma with his *The Case of Prison Monger*. I can't also forget my favourite, Evelyn Awuor Ayoda, with her *Workday*. It is a great book.

In History I liked European history, especially the history of the two Great Wars, and of course the other war, The Cold War. These wars made for an interesting study. They gave an impression of how European soil was turned into a stage for political alliances. In those years Europe staged the politics of 'Let's form a strong camp so that they will not knock us down.' Then the rival camps took each other to the battlefield. Those were the natives of Europe. The sons of Europe pointed their rifles at each other with their fingers on triggers. Then Boom! Boom! The guns fired. A tear-provoking smoke flooded over from

Europe into other lands. It *itched* the eyes of many non-Europeans.

That was history in a very far away land, a land across the Mediterranean Sea.

At home, history was being made, too. In 2011 in Malawi, it was the era of Dr. Bingu Wa Muntharika. In my Great Nation on the 20th of July of the same year, that is when it happened. Citizens took to the streets and rioted against the regime of Dr. Bingu Wa Muntharika. The masses were angry. They said there was human rights abuse: a lack of foreign currency, lack of fuel, you may name it.

So the black smoke erupted from the streets. There was a thick smoke. Boom! Boom! The police fired tear gas. A chant went:

Bingu Achoke!   Bingu step down!
Bingu Achoke!   Bingu step down!

That was 2011 in my Great Nation. In fact, I personally single out 2011 as a year of its own. It does not require extensive knowledge of political science for you to single it out as a year of political unrest around the globe.

Was it not the same year when Gadhafi was brought down from power in Libya after a bloody revolution? Was it not the same year when

America's "War on Terror" finally succeeded in killing the most wanted man on Earth, Osama Bin Laden, in Pakistan? Was it not the same year when a bloody revolution flared in Syria as the masses took to the streets to protest against the regime of Bashir Al Assad? Was it not the same year when the tension between Western Powers and Iran was rising to a climax? The Western Powers accused Tehran of building nuclear weapons.

CHAPTER TWENTY-SEVEN

As an amateur translator

In those days it was rainy. It must be the early days of a new year, around the early days of February.

I had graduated from Masongola Secondary School some few months earlier. I tried to apply to different colleges. I applied to a school of Journalism in Blantyre: the Malawi Institute of Journalism (MIJ). People told me they had heard my name called on the radio to get set for the school's entrance examinations scheduled on a later date.

But by then I had relaxed the muscle of my desire to go into journalism. In fact my heart had been drawn to African Bible College (ABC).

'It is an American standard school here in Malawi,' the late Joshua Likonde tried to drill into my ears. He was a close friend and a worker at the Passion Center. 'It has three campuses in Africa. One is in Uganda, another in Liberia. I encourage you to apply.' His words began to bear an effect on me. I left no newspaper unturned in case the ABC advertised a call for applications. When the ABC announced that they were accepting preliminary applications, I wrote a short autobiography and gave it to Joshua who submitted it online to ABC for me.

At times at home, I told my grandmother that I was planning to go to an American standard school. 'What will you speak back when they speak to you in their language, *Chizungu*?' she asked me when I cherished an idea to go to ABC before her.

'I know their language. I learnt it in school,' I replied with confidence. 'If I am able to speak with whites at the Passion Center, I will also be able to speak with whites at this school. English is English.'

As I was waiting for feedback, I was able to serve with the Community Health Network Ministry at the Passion Center. It was a community health support branch under the umbrella of the Passion Center. It was in its young life and led by Professor Sharon Christman from Cedarville University. In fact, she was the one who hatched the program under the Passion Center. I was still an amateur at translating, so I had a supervisor, Ireen. I stood in front with Sharon. It was my first attempt to stand in front for translation. I transferred the words from her tongue to our tongue. I was not that bad. Ireen came in wherever I needed assistance.

In that year Sharon worked with Matthew Wojnarowski. Together they trained some volunteers from the surrounding villages. The leader of the volunteers was Austin Chisuse.

On a later day, they trained them how to measure blood pressure with a stethoscope and a sphygmomanometer.

The sphygmomanometer had a cloth pad that was tied on your arm. It was tied just above the elbow. It had a hollowed pipe whose end had an elastic balloon. The balloon was oval shaped. On one end of the tube was a round metal piece that had some readings inside. In its midst stood a thin pointer with a sharp end.

The balloon was continuously pressed by hand. The cloth pad tightly gripped the arm. The stethoscope was put in the ears. It had a flat round metal disc. This metal was inserted in the cloth pad. It was all nice how the community volunteers mastered how to use the medical instruments. They tried to practice it on some members that came with Sharon's team.

On the last day of training, we went into the villages. The community volunteers carried their medicine boxes. The stethoscope and the sphygmomanometer were also brought. They cleaned the wounds and measured the blood pressure of the people we found in the villages. We also visited some sick people. The volunteers talked of a pending bicycle ambulance. This was to be provided soon to take the sick to the nearest hospitals.

We were done. We returned to the Passion Center. As we drew near lunchtime, Sharon said

'Prophet, you can come with us for lunch.' I liked the sound of that. I did not hesitate, and with energy I said 'Sure.'

So I jumped into the car and off we drove. There were three of us in the car; myself, Sharon and Matthew.

We drove to Tasty Bites. We found Jon Herman sitting in a chair. He was one of the missionaries who came with Sharon's team.

'Jon is here,' spoke Sharon as Matt packed the car.

'Yeah. Seen him,' replied Matt.

'Hello guys,' he greeted us. We got out of the car. We sat at one table. There were other *Azungu* at other tables. There was one thing that I experienced when I went out with whites to restaurants. You might think all whites at the restaurants know each other only to learn that they are also strangers to each other.

'What are you going to have?' asked Sharon after she had checked the menu. I cleared my throat continuously.

'Chips and chicken,' I said, my mouth salivating. As I was about to start eating, she suggested I could add some vinegar to my chips.

'It feels good when vinegar has been added,' she said.

In the months of June and July, the CHN was carried on by Dr Tracy Ricke. She worked together with Erika Beleen, a young graduate from University of Michigan. I also translated for them.

In fact, during this time I was able to translate for a number of people. I met David Kirkey, Justin Kirkey, Nate Maust, Heidi, Greig and Cheryl Kliech, Jacob Freeman, Zebulen E Dawson, Brenda and Kara Tiffan and Kim. These were Ohioans. With the Tiffans we held a vision clinic. People from surrounding villages came to the Passion Center and had their eyes examined. Some were given vision glasses. The vision clinic was also held in distant villages whose people could not walk to the Passion Center.

From California, I met the young Andy Durrenburg, Andy Weeks, Eric and his son Weston Sythoff, Mary Beachler and the Azusa Pacific University girls.

Yes, "the APU girls," as they were fondly called by the rest of the team. Among them were Lena Nomvo Vanda, Becky Johnson, Alex Robinson, Jayde Scott and Brittany Noelle Calsern. They stayed in Africa for some months and did many missionary works. They hired us to translate for them. It was a great experience. They taught the word of God, helped with school work and played games with kids from the Passion Center and the surrounding villages. On the last day of their work they held a slight feast with the kids.

And each kid went home with a picture with the APU girls on it. On the bottom of the left corner it read: AZUSA PACIFIC UNIVERSITY. While on the top of the right corner it read: OFFICE OF WORLD MISSIONS, DEVELOPING HEARTS AND MINDS FOR MISSIONS.

PART THREE

The Brighter Day

Before I learnt how to read and write, I thought a life of poverty was a normal life. But later, a black woman and some whites sent me to school to learn how to read and write. I have now unlocked the secret that a life of poverty is a captive life. The same happened to Fredrick Douglass, an American slave. He taught himself how to read and write. He mastered those skills and realized that slavery was not a normal life. He finally escaped. So boys and girls, stay in school and unlock the secret of your obstacle to a normal life.

CHAPTER TWENTY-EIGHT

I go to university

As my application to the African Bible College was still in the pipeline, I also sent an application to the University of Livingstonia, shortly abbreviated as UNILIA. It was a Christian university run by the Church of Central Africa Presbytery in the northern part of Malawi.

I applied for a place in the faculty of Social Science to specialize in Human Rights studies. Within a space of three weeks I received feedback. I was offered a place. I soon resolved to go and study at this school for I was unsuccessful in the African Bible College entrance examination. Pilira Chibwana phoned the ABC shortly after the ABC had released an intake list. I learnt that I did not make it.

UNILIA's academic calendar indicated that the arrival day was the 1st of September. Classes commenced on the 2nd of September, 2012.

I departed on the 31st of August. I travelled from the South to the North. This distance took a whole night by bus.

On the night of the 31st of August, I was on the bus. My whole attention was directed toward the front. There was a heated argument between some military officers, the female conductor and the driver. These were young officers and they had just completed a basic military training with the Malawi Armed Forces College. The officers accused the female conductor and the driver of being selfish. They said that they lacked customer care. The officers were drunk and they were standing in the corridors for the bus had run out of seats.

'I need a seat,' one officer said drunkenly.

'There is no seat left,' said the female conductor.

'No seat? What about that seat?' his friend asked.

'It is the driver's bed,' replied she without interest.

'That's nonsense and selfish. Why did you not refuse my money if you knew that the bus has run out of seats?'

'Okay. If you can't allow us to sit, at least give this woman a seat,' commanded the second officer. He pointed to a heavy woman in size who stood with them in the corridor.

'It can't happen,' the driver jumped in, having remained silent since the argument erupted. He was sitting on his bed. His turn to drive had not yet come.

'Hey, do not trouble the driver. He is going to carry many lives on this car. There are also the lives of young ones on this bus. He is a human like us and he feels offended,' spoke the conductor, trying to calm the situation.

'But he has no humanity. Why deny the woman a place to sit?'

'Mr. Driver, when I get home I will for sure go to a witch doctor and bewitch you,' jumped in the third officer.

'You are out of your senses little boy. Mind your tongue. Don't dig your own grave,' spoke the driver with energy. His bold voice filled the bus. It had grown silent in the bus. 'I was born in midst of the medicine that bewitches careless people like you. In my compound, waters that leave a bathroom are not wasted. It waters medicine,' he carried on. 'That's all that I can tell you.'

The argument went on as the two parties challenged each other on who knew more powerful medicine than the other, but it died away shortly as each officer, one by one, fell asleep soundly on the floor of the bus. And it was quiet, so quiet that one would not believe that, an hour or so earlier, it was the same bus that staged the stormy argument.

I arrived at the foot of the mountain. I was at Chitimba. I met other new students: Innocent and Maclean. On the roadside there was a post. The post was labeled "University of Livingstonia." A winding, dusty road crawled up the mountain. The way it wound, it took the shape of snake as it crawls on a rough floor. This was the famous road, *Gorodi*, dug by Robert Laws, a Scottish missionary. I learnt it from older students we found at Chitimba. Every time the sun shined, it shone because of its red earth.

This road had many stories attached to it as told by the older students I found at the foot of the mountain. Did we not hear that this road had seventeen sharp bends in total? Yes, we did. Did we not hear that the sharpest of all was Bend One? Yes, we did.

'Bend One. The famous bend,' they said proudly. It really made us feel like strangers. It set fear in us newcomers as they continued with their stories about Bend One.

'We all pray for repentance before passing by,' they would continue.

What about the Mantchewe Falls? This, too, they talked about. We learnt that one student had fallen into the roaring rapids and died.

We drove up the stony road. It was banked by tall green trees, and a gentle peaceful wind blew in the trees. As we drove up and up we saw steep and sloped edges that were formed as the road was being carved. Some edges were stony and sharp as they were formed from the scraped huge stones.

We saw many other things all along. After Bend Five as we drove from the bottom of the valley, and after Bend Four as we drove from the top of the hill, we reached a place called Holy Water. There was a running stream. It had some cold water. It was widely said that this was the place where Robert Laws quenched his thirst after the tiresome work of building the road.

    The bus came to a place where the road was covered with red earth throughout. It had some fine stones. The people's houses came into sight. We came to a post of the widely spoken-of Mantchewe Falls. The entrance was tightly closed-in with trees. The trees had broad leaves that cast a dense shadow on the ground. The post read `Welcome to Mantchewe Falls: Ancestral Cave and Nature`s Side.'

CHAPTER TWENTY-NINE

Back to the drawing board

The first two weeks were dedicated to orientation for the new students. We were being familiarized with our faculty and the whole campus.

The school had a mission statement: "THE UNIVERSITY OF LIVINGSTONIA, THROUGH EXCELLENCE IN TEACHING, RESEARCH AND LEARNING ENVIRONMENT, SHALL EDUCATE AND INSPIRE STUDENTS TO BECOME PRINCIPLED LEADERS WHO WILL TRANSFORM SOCIETY FOR THE GLORY OF GOD."

The Student Union executive members, Mike Theu, Jeremiah Nkowani, Maurice Tambala and Penelope Nyirenda, took us around the campus. They showed us as far as the Stone House and the old CCAP church. The Stone House was the house where Robert Laws used to stay before he returned to Scotland.

On top of the main entrance of the church was a very big glass with some paintings of people that were only visible when darkness fell. There was a White man that stood between two parties in the painting. The two parties were the people from Ngoni and Tumbuka tribes. A friend of mine and a poet, Lydia Tchongwe, told me that the painting represented the pacification and unity that the missionary Robert Laws brought between the warring Tumbuka and Ngoni people through Christianity.

My roommates were Abraham Pemba and Wakisa Mwenelupembe. They were both in the faculty of Education and in their final year.

In our class there were only eight of us. It was still in the early days of school and I made friends with Andy, Gift, Mwabi, Khumbolane and Naitara.

From other faculties I befriended Lindani Mughogho, Sarah Ackim, Owen Mchekeni and Mastano Dzimbiri. These were friends in the early days. And I should not also forget Innocent Lukhere, Laston Poi Gundani and my buddy Patrick Rabin Patel from the faculty of Applied Sciences.

Students from the English Department talked much about *Things Fall Apart* by Achebe. Of course I had once heard about the book from my uncle, James Mbewe, when he suggested I should read it someday for it was a great book. The fame of the book was gaining ground as the Literature students talked about it much. As beginners they were going to read this novel and the other one, *The River Between* by Ngugi Wa Thiong'o.

They started with Achebe's novel, so they talked about it a lot as they talked about some funny characters in the story. I was moved to read it and appreciated it myself. When I first opened the book and read the first line of the first chapter: '*Okonkwo was well known throughout the nine villages and even beyond,*' I attached the hero's fame to that of the book itself as its popularity flooded over to the other faculties on the campus.

I began reading it. I was glued to it. Then a thought came to my mind, out of nowhere it just struck my mind. 'Why don't I go to a class where they teach this book?' my mind began getting impregnated with the idea. 'It might be interesting,' I was obsessed. After digesting the thought, I 'tied a knot.' I was going to switch from the Faculty of Social Sciences to the Faculty of Education.

I went to the Dean of Faculty, Dr. J. Mlenga. She advised me to make some consultation with the Dean of Social Science first. His name was Matt Maroon from the USA.

'Yes young man,' he began happily. 'How may I help you?' By then we sat outside his office.

'I am planning to switch programs. I am going into the Faculty of Education,' I hammered the nail on the head.

'Are you sure of what you are saying?'

'Yes. Very sure,' said I with some nervousness. But I tried not to express it on my face or in my voice.

'Why?' his voice became so loud and clear. It became deathly still. I was thinking of the best answer to give him. Should I say I am interested in *Things Fall Apart*? No. I also supplied the answer. I was going to sound stupid. Hopefully he was going to say 'Why don't you read it in your spare time?

'I feel like I made a hasty decision to go into the faculty of social science,' I came in after the short break.

'Maybe you are also making the same hasty decision to switch,' he became so critical. 'Try to look into it from that way as well.'

'No. I am completely sure of the step I am taking now.'

'Sure?'

'Yes sir.'

'Look I am scared to give a final say. I might rush you into something. So think about it tonight and come back to me tomorrow'

I went away. When the next day came I went to see him. The new choice was still as solid as a melted metal which has just been cooled and when we met I put it in plain and simple language: 'I am switching.'

He wrote me a note to the University Registrar, Mr. W. Shaba. I withdrew my registration form. My new registration form indicated that I was going to study English, History and Theology and Religious Studies. Here I made a very important step for I chose Literature and History, where I was passionate. Previously, I had lost myself because I chose social science, which I was not passionate about, so I was an alien to it. Passion is the best source of happiness, creativity and innovation. And mostly innovative and creative minds move forward.

If our societies are to move forward, the education system must provoke passion and creativity in the minds of the learners. A good education system enriches the brain and makes it creative. And a rich and creative brain is a solid foundation on which national development powerfully stands. But a poor education system recreates the poverty of the brain. And the poor brain is a fertile ground on which national poverty breeds.

Yes. I set my feet in English Literature class. We were taught by Mr OC Mkandawire. In my new class they widely called him 'Shakespeare.' He had some baldness and was partly grey-haired on his sides of the head. He was also bearded. When lecturing he liked to caress his beard and then crack a joke. At times he dramatically caught a comb in his beard. He was a funny character.

I loved it in the following semester when he organized a Night of Oral Literature. He asked me, Kondwani and Becky to organize it.

On the night, we made a bonfire from a burning log. We sat around it. At the same time we roasted sweet potato, fresh maize and cassava.

As we roasted, we sang traditional songs and threw puzzling riddles. It brought me back to those old days, the days when I was a little kid in our compound.

`Ndagi!' the first person warned the others to prepare for a riddle

`Chize!' the audience showed preparedness.

`I have a house with no door,' threw the first person.

`Groundnuts,' someone tried to guess.

`No,' jumped in the one who threw. `Should I reveal?'

`No, we are still thinking over it.'

`An Egg!'

`Yes that's correct.'

Yes. That was the Night of Oral Literature.

In the same second semester, the University of Livingstonia Writers' Forum was hatched out. It was hatched out by OC Mkandawire, Miss Kawananga Kamanga and Albert Mtungambera Harawa. Mtungambera was a visiting Lecturer from Mzuzu University. He was teaching African and Diaspora Poetry.

It was through the writers' forum I was inspired to work on the first draft of a novel: 'From Exile.' It was my first attempt at a novel. Later the forum was joined by Ndongolera Mwangupili, a notable domestic writer and a visiting lecturer in Creative Writing at our university. I showed him the draft of my novel.

CHAPTER THIRTY

A People of the Rock

I got into mainstream translation when we were on school break. I translated either from a foreign tongue, English, into our tongue, Chichewa, or from our tongue into the foreign tongue.

My mainstream translation started with a team from Northwest Bible Church of Ohio. I might not be sure to say that the team's leader was Pastor Mark Trotter, but to my observation I may say he was. He was one of the pastors at this church.

I translated with the VBS at the Passion Center and the Child-Headed Households ministry. We also had a hospital visitation with them. We went to Zomba Central Hospital.

Before the Ohioans left, we had a team photo. For the first time I appeared in a team photo with the Passion Center staff and the missionaries. Each year a team photo was captured on a wide rock that stood maybe ten minutes walking from the Passion Center residence halls.

This rock was very famous to the missionaries who came to the Passion center. It was this same rock that my friend George Clearly

(Molly Clearly's father) joked about one day. He said the Passion Center family we are `A People of the Rock.'

In that year I was on the rock too, with the missionaries. I appeared with Pastor Eric Von Barnau Sythoff, Reverend Pilira Chibwana, Pastor Mark Trotter, Amy, Mr. Banda, Brian Buck, Uncle Titi, Uncle Stewart, Zach and Jake Balmet, Chris and Joni Weaver, Greig and Cheryl Kielich, David Kirkey, Nate Maust, Jeff McNeil, Mr. Kuntembwe, Sophie, Mr. Ntaja, Sarah Hamilton, The Demani brothers, Fatsani Mbewe, Caitlin, Mrs. Moses, Daniel Sutton, Mr. Lamusi, Allison Petit, Lena Vanda, Joshua Likonde, Fred Munkhondya, Karen Carter, Mrs. Jenala, Mrs. Majawa, Mrs. Dambo, Mrs. E Ntaukira, Mphatso Sekiya, Uncle Joe, Mrs. Nyerere, Molly Lalonde, Kathy Stagg Ward (mum), Connex Mwale, Corey Patterson, Jamie Dato, Mrs. Nkhoma, Polly Kishel, Jillian Cross and Jim Mtambo. It was a good experience. In fact you could not just wake up one day and say you were going to appear in the team photo. No, it was only for those who had served with the missionaries.

We were dressed in pink T-shirts. In front they had the image of Africa. The image of a tiny Malawi appeared somewhere in the southern part on the African map. At the back they were written: nwbible.org/missions.

The Californians flew in later and they picked up where the Ohioans had stopped. With them we added the reform school mission at Chilwa Reformatory Center.

I loved the Child-Headed-Households ministry so much. Under this ministry, the Passion Center looked after families where children were raising themselves as a family.

We travelled to a number of houses. I clearly recall we went to James Gomwa's house. Their village was located somewhere in Ulumba, and their house stood at the foot of a mountain. They were living by themselves, four brothers: James, Patrick, Bothwel and Mosses.

Their house was grass-thatched. Its walls, built from sun-dried bricks, had some huge cracks due to violent rains from the previous rainy season. The walls were weak.

At a distance, there were some newly molded bricks. It was a Passion Center project to build them a new house.

Next to James's house was Chimwemwe's. He was another kid living by himself. He was also under the Passion Center program through the CHH ministry.

Before the VBS started, the missionaries went into James's house. There was the clicking of cameras. At one point, the family was asked to stand in front of the house. And a photo was taken.

Kids from neighboring compounds were drawn to James' house. There was an open ground. Some few mango trees had broad leaves that cast shadows on the open ground. Uncle Stewart had his faithful guitar in hands now. The singing began. This song was very much liked by the missionaries. The song said that there was none like Jesus Christ. I had been to many places, I searched but still I can't find anyone to match Jesus Christ.

> *Palibe wofana naye!*
> *Palibe!*
> *Palibe wofana naye!*
> *Sazapezekaso!!*
>
> *Ndayendayenda*
> *Ponse ponse!!*
> *Ndazungulira*
> *Ponse ponse!*
> *Ndafunafuna*
> *Ponse Ponse!*
> *Sazapezekaso!!*

It was funny how everyone danced to its tune. At the chorus we uniformly walked a few steps forward. Then we rotated and finally searched with our hands.

After that we had a VBS with the kids. Where Abusa Fatsani or Titi did not stand in front with a missionary, I was the one translating. By then Titi was a CHH Coordinator and Fatsani worked in the Spiritual Department at the Passion Center.

After that we drove back. By then the ball of the yellow evening sun was slowly getting swallowed at the end of the Earth. The cameras were in motion as the missionaries excitedly captured the scene of the yellow sun sinking by the mountain. As we drove back, children ran in cleared gardens to wave at us. They were dirty and dressed in threadbare clothes. They looked unkempt. `Azungu! Azungu!' they ran excitedly as they waved with their hands.

Through the *Pajero's* window, I looked at the poor kids waving. I thought of them. By then each night before bed, I read a chapter or two of Legson Kayira's *I Will Try*. I thought of myself, Legson and those waving kids.

Legson was a village kid, dirty like them, but he walked on an epic trip to the USA to search for an opportunity. Myself, I was a village kid, dirty like them but here I was riding in a car with strangers. They were strangers who spoke a language different from mine. Their skin was also different from mine. And I was in their car because I had an opportunity. But what about these waving kids, did they realize that they were on a battlefield and individually had to make wise choices to successfully come out of the battlefield? Would they be privileged with the generous throwing an opportunity on their path? And will they be brave enough to realize such an opportunity and make use of it? It does not take for an ordinary human to capture an opportunity. Only unique and determined people can capture an opportunity.

I was still buried in the jungle of thoughts. My thoughts were provoked by those kids I saw as blind. They needed also to ride in the strangers' car to see beyond. I also thought if they could be able to read, they would have read a chapter or more in Legson Kayira's `I Will Try.' Like me, on reading the very last line of the last chapter, they would have taken a step ahead. It made me say: it is only when we have overcome our enemy in a fight that we claim victory in our hands. Mostly such a victory is a powerhouse for others fighting a similar war, somewhere. So they hang in the fight and claim the victory as well.

I was brought back to life when Kelly Hegelberg began to talk about jokes.

`Tell us Malawian jokes', she said.

`No, tell us American jokes.' So we cracked and cracked and cracked the jokes. The `Chicken joke' was cracked, too. Why did it cross the road?

'To get to the other side' was the answer. But I liked the 'knock knock joke' very much.

'Knock knock'

'Who is it?'

'Boo'

'Boo who?'

'Why are you crying?'

We all laughed. There were about six or seven of us in the car.

'Knock knock'

'Who is it?'

'Orange"

'Orange who?'

'Knock knock'

'Who is it?'

'Banana'

'Banana who?'

'Orange you glad I did not say banana.'

It stirred laughter in the car. As we laughed Desmond White passed a bottle of sanitizer. The bottle had a sticker with some words. *Germ X, Original Hand sanitizer, Kills 99.99% of germs.* We spread it in our hands and rubbed them.

Desmond was close to me just like Daniel Sutton. He was an African American. I remember on his first day at the Passion Center kids greeted him in our tongue as they thought he was a Malawian. I had thought the same too, but I learnt that he was not a Malawian from our first interaction.

The sanitizer was passed on. Desmond passed it on to Daniel Sutton, who passed it on to Becky Johnson, then to Musa Nyirenda, then to Lynsie, then to Kelly, then Marc Magana, then to me.

We drove following the car in front of us. It also belonged to our team. I am sure Nathan Jeffers was the one driving.

CHAPTER THIRTY-ONE

The growing inspiration

Back at the University I still enjoyed Literature classes. It was as if my heart had a hole, and every time I got into a Literature class, this hole got filled.

By then we were being taught by a young graduate, Ron Sichali. He had just completed his studies with the University of Botswana for his master's degree. I remembered him on one thing. He emphasized on being original in our works. His stylistic approach to literary pieces won my heart. He inspired me.

I showed him the script of my novel. It was a rough draft. He also showed it to Patricia Erdmann. She was from Washington and a visiting lecturer in Leadership and Management. Together (Ron Sichali, Patricia Erdman and Wezi Chiziwa) they were in the leadership of the writers' forum. I was the secretary of the forum while my roommate Mastano Dzimbiri was the president of the forum. My close friends and poets Fremings Mkanda, Kumbeni Chibweya and Maclove Kamba were also members of the forum.

In classes of this young graduate, I loved to get exposed to debates in the literary world. I liked the language debate in the African Novel class. In fact I personally love the academic ground when it comes to debates. It is an open ground where an idea is valued and looked at with respect.

Was it in 1962? Yes. It was at Makerere University. I loved to read from Ngugi Wa Thiong'o's *Decolonizing the Mind*. It was so exciting to go through the language debate.

Ngugi was for the vernacular as a medium through which an African writer should communicate. But Achebe stood on the other bank. He argued. Colonialism has misshapen African history and the clock cannot reverse. Yes, the British have given Africans the English language. Africans should exploit it by Africanizing it. That was the academic debate. It was very exciting to read and discuss the ideas these two African literary giants put forward on the endless language debate for African writers.

I also loved some of the debates in African and Diaspora Poetry. One erupted on 'Accommodation.' Some said black writers taken as slaves in America, the Harlem Renaissance writers, should be accommodated as Africans writers. Others were against this line of thought. They argued Black-American writers were not Africans. They were Americans so they could not be recognized as African writers.

Another debate was about Wole Soyinka's 'pouncing tiger' and the pioneers of the Negritude Movement. The black intellectuals from the

Western African French colonies, David Diop, Leopold Seghor and others, stood on the forefront to restore the pride in black culture they felt was diluted by European penetration in Africa. So the critic Wole Soyinka argued against the philosophy of the movement. "A tiger doesn't proclaim his tigritude," he argued. "He pounces."

So I loved to read about such debates. Such debates made for an interesting study especially when I personally reflect on how they have shaped an understanding of ourselves as Africans. In the scholarly world, debates have created powerful perspectives on which African scholars stand in search for a true African identity untarnished by the waves of slavery, missions and colonialism.

When we were almost done for the semester, I would look in advance the books we were going to read in the following semester. I would ask Ron to tell me the books so that I could fetch or read them during the holiday. In another semester we were going to read African American Literature.

So I messaged Kathy Stagg Ward. I was and still am fond of her.

'Mum, I need to tell you something?' that was I when I had punched the sign-in button to Facebook.

`Okay go ahead. In USA we say you are all ears,' she replied.

`Next semester we are reading African American Literature. So I am looking for Fredrick Douglass's *Narrative of the Life of Fredrick Douglass*; Harriet Jacob's *Incidents In The Life of A Slave Girl*; Olaudah Equiano's *The Life of Olaudah Equiano, or Gustavus Vassa, The African*; Booker T Washington's *Up From Slavery* and Orlando Patterson's *Slavery And Social Deaths*.'

`Are they the only works you are reading in the next semester?' she wanted to know.

`And of course Phyllis Whitley's *On Being Brought from Africa to America*; Cullen Countie's *Heritage*; Langston Hughes's *The Negro Artist and The Racial Mountain* and *Afro-American Fragments*. Not forgetting WEB DuBois' `Double Consciousness' and a philosophical debate between WEB DuBois and Booker T Washington.'

When the team came, Jamie Dato brought me a package with the items I had requested.

PART FOUR

The Endless Story

A kid in the village, in Africa, blindly thinks a life of poverty is a normal life. This kid needs an opportunity to stand on and look beyond to realize that poverty is not a normal life.

CHAPTER THIRTY-TWO

The needy need an opportunity

The stories are endless. Out of a million poor kids, I am one of the luckiest, for an opportunity has come my way. The path is full of a million kids in my situation. And seldom has an opportunity fallen on their path. Each of the kids has a story to tell. They first need a source of energy to voice out their stories. This source of energy is an opportunity that will help them realize that there is a better life. I tell my story today because I was given an opportunity once in my lifetime. From such an opportunity I have grown a strong muscle to tell my story with a pen and paper.

A poor kid does not need a fished-out fish. No, a fish will recreate poverty in a life of the poor kid. He or she needs an opportunity that will teach them how to use a fishing line.

That moment when you realize that this kid needs an opportunity, that is when you qualify as a game changer. The desire to bring change originates from the very core of the heart. This desire will always have profound effects.

Blessed are those who throw an opportunity on the path of those who need it for they create a stepping stone for the betterment of this world. As humans of the 21st Century we have two options for this world. We either we make it a better place or a worse place to live.

And to fellow kids, names known and names unknown, travelling the path I did, realize that an opportunity is just a stepping stone. The greatest achievement your mind can make is to discover that an opportunity is just there for you to step on and proceed. Foolish is the person who is blind to a life beyond an opportunity. But clever is the person who realizes that an opportunity will just help him or her to jump to a life beyond the opportunity.

I will offend you if I do not reveal that an opportunity is one of the most fragile things in this life. It is brittle, very brittle, and it easily breaks into a million tiny pieces. These pieces cannot be glued back together easily.

If you have an opportunity, cushion it and take full advantage of it.

(My prayer goes to the Passion Center for Children Organization and Africa at large)

A GLOSSARY OF LOCAL TERMS

Amanda	: Spirits of the dead
Anamkungwi	: Female initiation elder
Anganga	: Grandmother
Azungu	: White people
Boma	: Colonial legal system
Bwalo	: The chief's ground
Chabulika	: A female initiation
Chibelemuda	: Game played on mud
Chigumu	: An African cake
Chitekwere	: Female initiation dance
Chizungu	: English language
Futali	: Cassava and nuts
Jando	: Male initiation
koloboyi	: Paraffin lamp
Kothopola	: Scavengers
Mjigo	: Village well
Mkate	: Banana bread
Mwinimbumba	: Head of family line
Nduna	: Messenger of the chief
Ngumbi	: Small white-winged ant
Nsima	: Thick porridge
Nyamu	: Small black-winged ant
Nyau	: Male initiation dancer
Simba	: Initiation shelter

Phada	: Game played on mud
Thobwa	: Sweet beer
Uta wa Leza	: Rainbow
Yesu	: Jesus
Yesu Kristu	: Jesus Christ